WHEN GOD BURSTS IN

REVIVAL
THEN
AND
NOW

Peter LUNDELL
and Elaine PETTIT

Beacon Hill Press of K
Kansas City, Miss

D1410134

Copyright 2005
by Beacon Hill Press of Kansas City

ISBN 083-412-2138

Printed in the
United States of America

Cover Design: Ted Ferguson

10   9   8   7   6   5   4   3   2   1

To the people of my church, and every other, who hunger for God

"LORD, I have heard of your fame;
I stand in awe of your deeds, O LORD.
Renew them in our day,
in our time make them known;
in wrath remember mercy."
—Hab. 3:2

CONTENTS

FOREWORD

ALL TRUE CHRISTIANS yearn for the revitalizing times when by God's majestic grace, the Holy Spirit renews the Body of Christ with fresh wind and fresh fire. Peter Lundell and Elaine Pettit have written an insightful, prophetic message calling us to embrace the genuine revival that God yearns to pour out on the Church today. The authors draw from extensive research and from an evangelist's life experiences to point the way to an invigorated, Spirit-ignited movement in our ever-changing world. They show us the history of revivals from biblical days to the present and challenge us to humbly embrace God's movement among us. Thrilling narratives and testimonies inspire the heart as we dare to believe that we could witness a mighty Kingdom-come occurrence in our generation.

Peter and Elaine desire to see believers experience the powerful transforming God-moments in their lives and also become fully devoted, Spirit-filled disciples of our Lord. They offer the believer and the local congregation a humbling tool that will help us evaluate qualitatively the condition of our personal spiritual life and that of our church. We often place most of our emphasis on prescribing or describing how a person enters into the experience of entire sanctification and fail to accentuate the equally important lifelong passion of maturing into the very likeness of our Lord. Authentic heart holiness is not primarily evidenced by our verbal testimony but by our life!

The authors quote J. Edwin Orr's teaching regarding three significant distinctions in the manifestations of the Spirit of God. God's initial work is an *outpouring*. Committed believers partnering with God spark *revival* in the church. God's prevenient grace working through a revived church will lead to an evangelistic *awakening*, where many lost people embrace saving faith in Christ. We know God is active in our world today. Spiritual resurgence will come when we are willing to humble ourselves, pray, study God's Word, and confess our sins. We confess to each other and to our Heavenly Father our sins of spiritual apathy; prayerlessness; materialism; lethargy in witnessing; secularism; losing our first love; and indifference to widows, orphans, and those in need. Renewal will come as we passionately cry out for God's fresh anointing.

Some think of revival as an event that will "revive" a past era. Authentic revival does take us back to the message and essence of the gospel but not always to the forms and methods of yesteryear. God usually breaks through by mobilizing the young adult generation who take the church by storm, revitalizing and reenergizing it with new passion, new music, and new methods. One reason revival does not come is because we yearn for the comfort of our past rather than bravely embracing the exhilarating unknown future where God is in control!

As we prayerfully read this book, may we covenant to be radically obedient to the Spirit's voice. May we so abandon ourselves to the Kingdom that God's prevenient outpouring becomes a mighty revival, which in turn becomes a precious global awakening allowing literally millions to become fully devoted followers of our Lord Jesus Christ!

—Jerry D. Porter
General Superintendent
Church of the Nazarene

PREFACE

I AM THRILLED to have one of America's leading Holiness evangelists joining me in writing this book. Elaine Pettit has a proven record of being an amazing instrument in God's hands. She travels full-time, knows how to get people to pray, and regularly witnesses the outpouring of the Spirit. In sidebars throughout the book she will share meditations on revival and seeking God. Then, in chapters 8 and 9, she will tell us from her own experience and that of others what the Lord is doing in churches today and how you and your church can pray more effectively.

As I researched and worked on this book, I could almost feel in myself the impact of the Holy Spirit's work in those who gave their testimonies. I refer not to just a movement or a revival. This is about the transformation of individual lives. It is about countless sinners saved and saints transformed. It is about local congregations electrified and new ones starting everywhere. Revivals have been real, life-changing experiences for hundreds of thousands—and now millions—of people. If any from the Holiness revival were here today, they would plead with us to lay aside everything we have and all we are doing to pursue the outpouring of the Holy Spirit. Nothing else compares.

The more I learned about our Holiness tradition, the more I fell in love with the Church of the Nazarene and other Holiness churches. As you read this book, celebrate our glorious past with Elaine and me. But never stay there. God gives us the past to instruct us about the future. In seeing what the Holiness revival and the resulting Holiness Movement was, we can see what it can be. The same Holy Spirit is working now as then, but today we live in a much different world. So we can expect the Spirit's work to be fundamentally the same, but we should also expect some of it to be new and different.

The future is ours to forge. Will you keep your eyes forward and upward? Will you keep your mind open and your heart humble and receptive to what the Lord would do in your own life and our own time? Will you pay the price in God-hungry prayer for receiving His work?

—Peter Lundell

WHEN GOD BURSTS IN

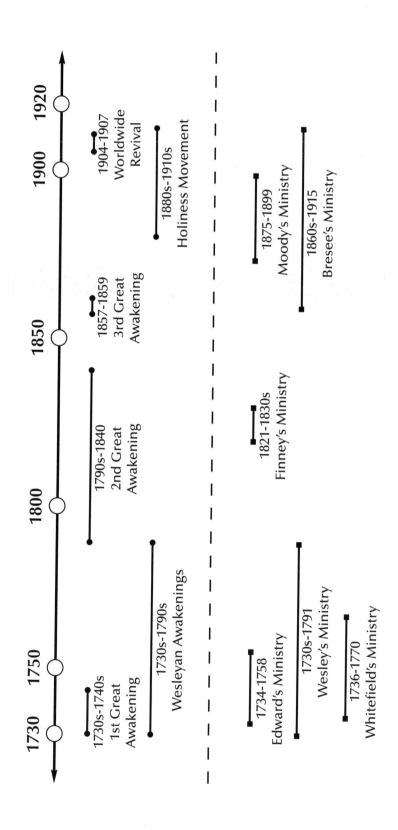

Timeline of Major Revivals and Awakenings

1730 1750 1800 1850 1900 1920

1730s-1740s
1st Great
Awakening

1730s-1790s
Wesleyan Awakenings

1790s-1840
2nd Great
Awakening

1857-1859
3rd Great
Awakening

1880s-1910s
Holiness Movement

1904-1907
Worldwide
Revival

1734-1758
Edward's Ministry

1730s-1791
Wesley's Ministry

1736-1770
Whitefield's Ministry

1821-1830s
Finney's Ministry

1875-1899
Moody's Ministry

1860s-1915
Bresee's Ministry

INTRODUCTION

"EVERY SUNDAY MR. HECKER ran up and down the center aisle waving his hands and praising the Lord. He was filled with the Holy Spirit. The whole church was filled with the Holy Spirit. I can still hear him shouting 'Hallelujah!' He often took off his coat and threw it over the clock so no one could tell what time it was. He didn't want the service to end." Now crooked and wrinkled, Dorothy smiled at her childhood memory and nodded with approval. The service she talked about, the one Mr. Hecker didn't want to end, was the Sunday morning worship. Every week, I looked up at the clock—a different one from Mr. Hecker's time, generations before—but a clock just the same. Our services at the Alhambra Church of the Nazarene never ran overtime. I now wish they had.[1]

The infilling of the Holy Spirit—let's go the whole way—the invasion of the Holy Spirit into a person's life or the life of a church congregation never happens just because we'd like it to. It happens because we hunger for God. And it happens because God chooses to graciously lavish himself on us. He does it in different ways at different times.

Does He still do it? Evangelist Elaine Pettit remembers an experience that happened in July 1994 at Lafayette Church of the Nazarene, in Lexington, Kentucky. The pastor wanted her to preach one more day than what she was scheduled, and she agreed.

During her personal prayers the next day, "deep sobs began to well up within" her as she sensed God's presence. Bill Bright describes a similar experience:

> While I was seeking His guidance, something extraordinary happened. I distinctly sensed a sobbing in my spirit and, amazingly, I knew our Lord was weeping. I was startled at first. And although I did not know why He was weeping, I began to sob,

13

too. Then I sensed Him saying, "My people have forgotten one of the most important disciplines of the Christian life, the major key of revival." And I knew He meant fasting with prayer.[2] Scripture expresses this in Rom. 8:26: "In the same way, the Spirit helps us in our weakness. We do not know what we ought to pray for, but the Spirit himself intercedes for us with groans that words cannot express."

Elaine believed that God was grieving over His Church and wanting her to remind His people that He is a holy God whose people must also be holy. Because they have lived lives of compromise and strayed from the narrow way, they must now humble themselves, pray, and repent.

That night the Holy Spirit ignited a revival. For the next 36 days and 42 services, many people testified to being saved, sanctified, and delivered. A large number were baptized, several testified to physical healings, and many were called to full-time ministry. Reconciliation occurred among the people, and some made restitution for wrongs as far back as 20 years.

Should we be amazed? Didn't God say, "If my people, who are called by my name, will humble themselves and pray and seek my face and turn from their wicked ways, then I will hear from heaven and will forgive their sin and heal their land" (2 Chron. 7:14)?

Elaine's experience is a preview of what God expects and what I hope will sweep churches across our nation. Will you read this book just for amusement or to pass the time? Or will you take it to heart and apply it? It could be a part of God changing your life and the life of your local church. What then is the best way to apply it?

QUALITATIVE MEASURING GAUGES

Lip service is the cheapest and easiest service in the world. Even God laments over the lip service of those who believe in Him: "These people come near to me with their mouth and honor me with their lips, but their hearts are far from me" (Isa. 29:13). Of all the services the Christian Church has ever held, lip service has been the best attended. Every positive change the Church ever had was when people got out of the lip service and into the doing service. In which one do you spend most of your time?

To make positive changes and to know where we're going, we should clarify where we're starting from and where we genuinely want, and will pay the price, to go. To do that it helps to qualitatively measure the state of our spirituality.

Qualitative measures (such as assessing the spiritual health of a church) are by nature more difficult to assess than quantitative measures (such as counting how many people attend a church). The first parallel gauge below attempts to help you qualitatively assess the condition of your own spiritual life; the second, the spiritual state of your own local church. You may find them incomplete as they relate to you or your church specifically. If so, feel free to add assessment questions of your own.

The scores on each gauge are not meant to be added up. Assess yourself and your church on the gauges to find areas where you and your church are doing well and where you and your church could change or improve.

Personal Life

1. Would Jesus say that I am walking in holiness, with a pure heart of love toward Him?

My life is not as holy as it ought to be.

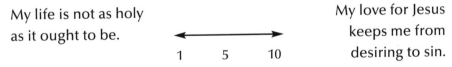

My love for Jesus keeps me from desiring to sin.

2. Is my life of holiness characterized more by living according to rules or a relationship?

I live by obeying rules that God would have me follow.

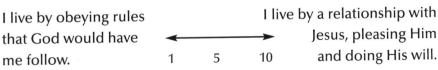

I live by a relationship with Jesus, pleasing Him and doing His will.

3. How much desire (spiritual hunger) do I have for the presence of God in my own life?

I pray a few minutes
each day.

I spend extended
periods, even hours,
in prayer.

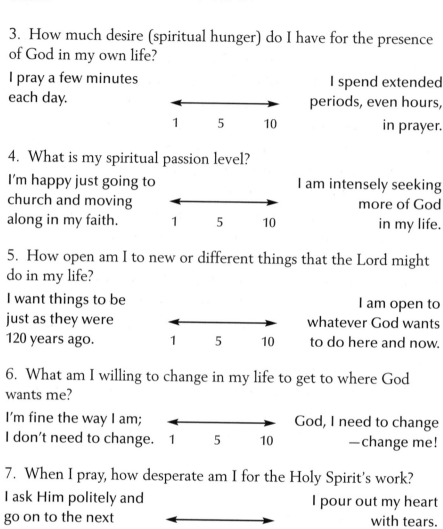

1   5   10

4. What is my spiritual passion level?

I'm happy just going to
church and moving
along in my faith.

I am intensely seeking
more of God
in my life.

1   5   10

5. How open am I to new or different things that the Lord might do in my life?

I want things to be
just as they were
120 years ago.

I am open to
whatever God wants
to do here and now.

1   5   10

6. What am I willing to change in my life to get to where God wants me?

I'm fine the way I am;
I don't need to change.

God, I need to change
—change me!

1   5   10

7. When I pray, how desperate am I for the Holy Spirit's work?

I ask Him politely and
go on to the next
prayer item.

I pour out my heart
with tears.

1   5   10

8. _____

Church Life

1. Would Jesus say that my church is promoting holiness, with a pure heart of love toward Him?

My church tolerates a
lot that it shouldn't.

Love for Jesus keeps
most of us from
desiring to sin.

1   5   10

2. Is my church's holiness characterized more by following rules or by a relationship with Jesus?

Our holiness is based on obeying rules God would have us follow.	←——————→ 1 5 10	Our holiness is based on loving and following Jesus.

3. How much does my church really want to see God manifest himself in our midst?

Our prayer meetings are fairly perfunctory and predictable.	←——————→ 1 5 10	Our prayer meetings are intense, passionate, and from the heart.

4. What is my church's spiritual passion level?

My church seems settled in its routines, even complacent.	←——————→ 1 5 10	People intensely seek a greater presence and work of God.

5. How open is my church to new or different things that the Lord might do among us?

My church holds to the ways things traditionally have been.	←——————→ 1 5 10	My church is open to whatever God wants to do here and now.

6. What is my church willing to change to get to where God wants us?

My church is fine the way it is; no need for change.	←——————→ 1 5 10	God, my church needs to change—change us!

7. When my church people pray, how desperate are we for the Holy Spirit's work?

We ask Him politely and go on to the next prayer item.	←——————→ 1 5 10	We pour out our hearts with tears.

8. _____

1

GLORY DAYS
The Holiness Movement

EVANGELIST LAWRENCE HICKS had preached for a week and had a good crowd but mediocre results at a Methodist church in the Cumberland Mountains. He tells the story of the surprising work of the Holy Spirit in that place. "On this Saturday night I preached, made an altar call, did all I was able to do as we sang three invitation songs through. Not one single person came forward. This being the closing service of the schedule, I prepared to dismiss the congregation."

Before he could do this, a man in the back of the sanctuary, who had been weeping and talking to his backslidden son, pleaded with Hicks, "Brother Hicks, please ask them to sing one more song." So they did. Then,

> with the suddenness of lightning, at about midway through the first stanza, the "break" came. The young man started toward the altar. A rather large man seemed stricken in the middle aisle. With tears streaming down his cheeks he sat in the middle of the aisle vowing that he would never budge until he had salvation; meanwhile people trampled him underfoot as if oblivious to his presence.
>
> In less than one minute the altar could hold no more seekers.

After these heart-stricken people had trampled on each other to reach the altar Saturday night, Hicks returned to his own church for Sunday morning services and agreed to come back one last night. He gives this report of what he saw when he neared the church on Sunday evening:

> When I came in sight of the church I was confronted with a multitude. I had to park my car at some distance from the church and walk to the building. The house was so filled that I with some difficulty reached the platform. I inquired of the state of affairs. I was informed that the congregation had met for Sunday school in the morning and the work of the Spirit had again broken out until they were unable to have Sunday school at all, but had engaged the whole day in praying souls through to victory in Jesus. . . . With no singing or preaching I gave immediately another invitation.[1]

When God comes in power, He shoves all our human efforts aside, overwhelming us with His presence. Have you tasted the unspeakable blessing of the Holy Spirit's bursting onto a church? Have you ached with the heart-gripping desire of that evangelist or that father to see someone saved or changed? Amazing movements of the Holy Spirit can appear almost anywhere at any time. They transform individuals, churches, regions, and even entire nations. They will happen again. I hope you can experience them.

Before we see firsthand testimonies of amazing works of God, let us see how they fit in the overall history of Holiness teaching and experience through the centuries.

HOLINESS THROUGH THE CENTURIES

From the Book of Leviticus through the New Testament and throughout church history, holiness has risen again and again as the prominent issue in the Christian life. In the 7th century, Maximus the Confessor saw "holiness as a profound liberation of the human psyche, a growing into the image of God."[2] In the late 16th and early 17th centuries, Jeanne Guyon ministered widely in France, teaching believers to be totally abandoned to God. She explained that "God wishes to make your soul pure. He purifies it by His Wisdom just as a refiner purifies metal in the furnace."[3] George Fox, the 17th-century founder of the Society of Friends (Quakers), emphasized "a non-doctrinal personal piety in which communion with God means everything."[4] Pietists, participants in a spiritual renewal movement originating in German Lutheranism, rose up against the pervasive institutional dryness and doctrinal controversies of their time to favor a deeper, personal relationship with Jesus Christ. A lifestyle of holiness and a pursuit of godliness were central to all they taught and lived.

Many of these Holiness mentors influenced John Wesley. After rough beginnings, with blunders and struggles, God transformed his life. For the next 50 years God used him to preach in every corner of Great Britain and raise sanctified believers, preachers, small groups, churches, and the massive Methodist movement, which transformed Great Britain, North America, and other parts of the world! The Holiness Movement as we know it is deeply rooted in Wesley and the Great Awakening of the 1730s and onward.

Phoebe Palmer, a Methodist laywoman in New York, picked up the spiritual torch in 1835 with her Tuesday Meetings for the Promotion of Holiness. She was the main historical link between Wesley and the Holiness Movement, as she promoted the experience, language, and theology of entire sanctification and the life of holiness. Charles Finney also emphasized holiness in his teaching at Oberlin, Ohio. But his view on holiness had more to do with human decision and lifestyle than with the grace of God.

After the American Civil War, Methodist Episcopal leaders formed the National Camp Meeting Association for the Promotion of Christian Holiness. This was the beginning of the resurgence of camp meetings that had so impacted the American frontier expansion in the early 1800s. Some consider the forming of this association to be "the beginning of the modern Holiness Movement in the United States, since within 40 years it resulted in the formation of over a hundred Holiness denominations throughout the world."[5]

Despite the importance of the National Camp Meeting Associ-

> Are you lacking even in only one area? Today, if you hear His voice, if you are not 100 percent sure that you are 100 percent right with God, tonight is the night to get it right.
>
> Nearly 100 percent came to the altar with weeping, and crying out, and praising our God in Christ Jesus. The Holy Ghost came, and how the fire fell! Many got it right with God. They were sanctified wholly!
>
> —Dr. Neal Gray's journal review of the revival campaign held at the Baltimore Parkview Church of the Nazarene, Baltimore, Maryland, May 4-7, 2002

ation, the Holiness Movement did not start with any one person or at any one place. The fire of the Holy Spirit spontaneously fanned out from one place to another. Generally accepted dates for the bulk of the movement that influenced North America start around 1880 and taper off around 1910. It was widely known to the general public and recognized by secular magazines, such as the *Philadelphia Home Journal*, which published a report proclaiming, "The whole Northwest is in a blaze of salvation. Holiness is the theme in every direction. . . . I have heard that ministers have gone home covered with sanctified power, and whole churches are at the altar seeking holiness."[6]

The movement spawned countless Holiness groups, most of which united with others to form the Holiness denominations we know today, such as the Free Methodists, the Salvation Army, the Wesleyans, and the Church of the Nazarene. Other churches, with different roots, have flowed into the same stream, such as the Church of God (Anderson), the Brethren in Christ, and the Evangelical Friends.

The Holiness revival and its ensuing movement created, defined, invigorated, and sometimes fractured whole denominations. The 1872 annual report of the National Camp Meeting Association made this statement about the revival: "Never before in the history of Christianity has there been so great and widespread an interest in this important subject as within the last four or five years. All denominations have been so aroused as to assure the most skeptical that this is truly the 'work of God.'"[7]

TESTIMONIES OF THE HOLY SPIRIT'S WORK

God wants to pour His Spirit onto a thirsty, seeking Church! Yet in many congregations descended from the Holiness Movement questions and cries rise up, sometimes spoken, sometimes unspoken. The quiet cries of many hearts sound like this: "Where is this great movement of the Spirit across the Church?" "Where is this overwhelming work of God in my own life?" Too often, with a lack of the Holy Spirit's work, people revert to a holiness of enforced lifestyle, that is, rules. The holiness of the movement that swept and changed the nation was a holiness of heart. Sinners didn't get saved and Christians didn't get holy just because the preacher told them to. They were saved and made holy because the Holy Spirit invaded their lives. As a boundary, rules are necessary; as a motivation, rules are oppressive. The work of the Spirit in what we call the Holiness Movement was not the controlled directive of a church organization; it was the Spirit of Jesus transforming lives. Only later were the boundaries (rules) added for the necessary definition of church life.

Holiness churches were born and multiplied on the waves of the Holiness Movement. The histories of their formation and growth are well known and available to anyone who wants to read them. But what did the Holy Spirit actually do in the very real lives of individual people? And what actually happened in their church gatherings? A July 4, 1899, all-day meeting at Los Angeles First Church of the Nazarene found new converts standing to testify of God's work in their lives. As they did, "The Holy Ghost fell upon the people in Pentecostal fashion, and probably fifty persons were on their feet at once praising God. The old patriarchs, with streaming eyes, rushed into each other's arms, giving glory to Jesus, the young converts waved their palms of victory, many shouted, and all gave themselves up to the mighty tide of glory and power."[8]

Does that sound like your church? If not, wouldn't you like to move closer to that experience? Do you hunger for it? Long for it? Pray for it? Will you open yourself up to the Holy Spirit for it?

To ignite future outpourings, or even increased activity of the Holy Spirit, we would be wise to recapture what the Holy Spirit did in the past. I don't mean we should try to duplicate it (we can't anyway). I mean we should grasp what the Spirit actually did. Later we'll see what He is doing now. This will inform us to be wise and inspire us to be passionate. The best way to grasp this is to absorb firsthand testimonies. Take a look with me at just a few out of countless testimonies from early Nazarene and other Holiness churches.

Personal Transformations

Personal testimonies from people touched by the power of the Holy Spirit characteristically have an abundantly joyful, emotional tone, such as this one:

> I was getting desperate; for the devil had cheated me long enough. I gave up all and received Him. He sanctified my heart and filled me with Himself. He has given me an aim in life, a marvelous object in living, to bring precious souls to Him. As the sunshine of His love streams into my heart more wonderfully every day, I can only wonder, and love, and praise. I praise Him for my blessed home in this Nazarene Church. It is the most sacred spot on earth to me. What a place to bring the wandering ones, where they are loved and shielded and held up to the Throne of Grace. Oh, it is wonderful. I never saw anything like it. I feel as though I had passed into a new world. If this is so blessed, what will be over there?[9]

Testimonies, like this one from Los Angeles, express the often-overwhelming work of the Spirit on the person's inward nature:

I want to tell you what the Lord has done for me. I have such peace and joy as only the sanctified know. O hallelujah to the Lamb of God that taketh away the sin of the world! The Lord has taken from me all worldly desires, left only a purpose of heart to serve Him in spirit and truth as long as I live. I am getting better established on the solid rock. Bless the Lord forever. "There is joy in my soul today." I am loving Jesus more and trusting him more all the time. When God saved me, He took all the desire for tobacco away. Bless His holy name forever. It is just wonderful what the Lord will do for sinners when they give themselves up in real earnest.[10]

Testimonies of new converts abound, and these converts often influence others to turn to Christ, such as this one:

Dr. Prime tells us of a boy who gave his heart to God at the Sabbath school, and early on the following morning he came to his parent and said, "Oh, father, my dear father, I have not been able to sleep all night, for I ought to have prayed with you before I went to bed, and I did not; do kneel down with me, and I will pray with you now." The father was astonished, for he himself was not a praying man, but he could not resist the pleadings of the boy. The father's heart was melted, and soon the father and two brothers were brought to the Saviour.[11]

Relational and Socioeconomic Impact

Seth Rees, early leader of the Pilgrim Holiness Church, for years led a tremendous urban ministry in Providence, Rhode Island. Here is just one summary report. Note the entire social range of the Spirit's work as well as the depth of individual transformations:

What a glorious year! Hundreds of drunkards, gamblers, harlots, and common sinners, as well as mechanics, bankers, merchants and church members, have been gloriously saved. . . . Many drunkards have not only been saved from rum, licen-

In the evening service, a young married man staggers into the service with assistance from the Associate Pastor. This is the first time the young man has ever been to the Lafayette Church. He falls down upon the altar and a great band of prayer warriors surround him with prayer. He is sobered up and saved in less than 15 minutes. He then testifies. . . . He states that he . . . has been an alcoholic since he was 13 years old—for 25 years.

—Pastor David McCracken's journal of the Lexington Lafayette Church of the Nazarene, Lexington, Kentucky, revival titled: "Spontaneous Outpouring of Holy Ghost and Fire—Fifty Days of Pentecost— July 3—August 21, 1994," 15.

tiousness and tobacco, but their bloated and diseased bodies have been healed, their faces freed from rum blossoms, and their wrecked, ruined lives made entirely new.[12]

In Sherburn, Minnesota, God convicted church people of their thievery of animals. Sanctification thus led to the righting of wrongs, including the restoration of broken relationships and financial compensations:

A woman prominent in church work flounced out mightily stirred, walked the floor all night fighting back conviction, but at last she yielded and gave her heart to God. About the first thing she did was to visit a neighbor and offer to pay for two chickens that her boys had stolen and brought home, that she cooked and helped eat. She declared that they were scratching in her stomach yet and she wanted the matter settled. Sunday she stood before her Sunday school class and asked them to forgive her for being such a hypocrite all these years. We left her with the glory in her soul and the shine on her face.[13]

Impact on Churches

Most significant testimonies were from churches, where the need for revival was often the greatest. Churches that scheduled revival meetings usually had them over a weekend or, if they were ambitious, for a whole week. Listen to this from Peoria, Illinois, in 1908: "This is the 15th week of the meeting, and it seems as if it had just begun; our hall is crowded, and the people fill the streets in front of the building, to hear the true gospel."[14] The 15th week! Imagine your church having revival services for 15 weeks—and to feel as if you were just starting.

The Chicago Church of the Nazarene, organized by Phineas Bresee, was also a hotbed of holiness. The presence of God displayed through the power of the Holy Spirit in that place at that time is awe-inspiring. The daylong crowds of people attested to the reality of the Lord's work:

> Immense crowds jammed the church, morning, afternoon and night. There were penitents at each of the services, including the Young People's meeting. The pastor preached the third in a series of sermons on "Entire Sanctification" in the morning. In the afternoon a class of twenty-six new members was received, amidst the shouts and rejoicings of the people. This makes seventy-five who have been received since the beginning of the present pastorate, or since the first of the year.[15]

Bresee gave this report of the Chicago Church of the Nazarene:

> The Nazarenes in Chicago love God with an ardor and intensity that is indescribable. They give expression to this burning love in varied ways. They smile and laugh and weep, and clap and wave their hands, and sing and shout, they say, "Amen," "glory," "hallelujah," "Bless God," "Praise the Lord," and other things which have ample scriptural warrant and sanction. Sometimes when they cannot help it, they leap for joy, and walk up and down the aisles or platform.[16]

He goes on to describe the amazing way in which people stayed at church from morning till night, with the Holy Spirit at work the whole time:

> They love one another with a warm, tender, and sincere af-
> fection, and do not permit differences of opinions to estrange
> them. . . . Sunday is a real camp meeting. Many scores of peo-
> ple come to the church in time for Sunday school, at 9:00
> A.M., and stay until 10:00 o'clock at night. They bring their
> food with them, and eat two meals in the church. . . . Now and
> then, even at these times, a soul is brought to the altar, and
> saved and sanctified.[17]

Try to imagine people staying at your church all day and into the
night and bringing not one but two meals with them! Can you see
the Holy Spirit convicting people for salvation or sanctification
during your church potluck dinner?

We're used to missionaries telling about the amazing things
God is doing on the foreign mission fields, while the churches in
North America sit and listen politely. An early Nazarene missionary
to India found it the opposite in 1906 while visiting America. After
a brief stay in Chicago she wrote, "It is hard to break away from
this enthusiastic church and people, who are all on fire with glory
from the skies, and they will push full salvation to the gates of the
enemy."[18] I hunger for that kind of presence of God. Don't you?

The Spirit's Work as an Attraction

At least one prominent center of the Holiness Movement even
became a tourist attraction. We still find this today. When God rais-
es a new movement of people who have great enthusiasm, commitment, and a powerful experience of the Holy Spirit, other curious believers will make sure to visit. Out-of-town tourists will put
it on their "must visit" itinerary. This is not to see beautiful archi-
tecture or a well-known institution. This "must visit" is where the
Holy Spirit is powerfully manifest in church gatherings and the
personal lives of believers. Wouldn't you love your church to be on
someone's "must visit" list? Los Angeles First Church of the Nazarene was, as these examples show:

> A company of tourists one day, leaving the city for their

eastern homes, were overjoyed to tell what they had seen in Los Angeles, and one of them asked: "Did you go to the Church of the Nazarene?" The other answered, "No, we heard about it, and intended to go, but in some way were hindered." The first rejoined: "Well, you ought to have gone. You never saw anything like it. The people sang and shouted and stood up and said they were sanctified, and it was the greatest thing you ever saw."

On one occasion a gentleman secured a bus and driver to show him the sights of the city. Among other places, he was taken to the Church of the Nazarene.[19]

The bewildered gentleman didn't quite know how to respond to the bus driver. The Nazarene church building he stopped in front of was not a grand cathedral; it was the so-called Glory Barn, the very flimsy first building the church ever had. But the Holy Spirit knew the place very well and spent a lot of time there. The driver knew it was worth a stop.

Wouldn't you want your church to be a landmark in your city? Wouldn't you want it known as a place where lives are changed?

FIRE-KINDLING QUESTION

Which testimony from this chapter grabs you most? What price would you pay before God for that testimony to become your own?

2
UNIVERSALS OF REVIVAL
Things True of Every True Revival

"WE'RE HAVING REVIVAL!" I have heard it many times. You've probably heard it too. Or perhaps more common is the heartfelt plea, "We're praying for revival!" What is a revival? When we report revival, what are we really reporting? When we pray for revival, what are we really praying for?

TRUE REVIVAL

Getting excited and proclaiming the wonders of God does not constitute a revival. Revivals have never started with joy. They have always started with the conviction of sin. The conviction of sin then leads to salvation, sanctification and empowerment, and the transformation of the church and hopefully the surrounding society. With this then comes great joy. Testimonies from revivals also speak of a great hunger for God expressed in the desire and burden to pray and of a heightened sense of God's presence among His people.

Here's a definition of revival from the early Holiness Movement: "A true revival of religion is a movement among the people produced by the power of the truth and the agency of God's Spirit, resulting in the quickening of God's children and the conversion and reformation of sinners."[1]

OUTPOURING, REVIVAL, AND AWAKENING

J. Edwin Orr makes three distinctions in understanding the manifestation of the Spirit of God as it relates to people: outpourings, revivals, and awakenings. "Outpourings of the Spirit are exclusively the work of God; but revivals are the work of God with the response of believers; awakenings are the work of God with the response of the people."[2]

Joel prophesied the outpouring of the Holy Spirit, saying, "I will pour out my Spirit on all people" (2:28). The Day of Pentecost in Acts 2 was a pouring out of the Spirit. People experienced the supernaturally manifest presence of God, and thousands of lives were changed. When the Holy Spirit works extraordinarily among believers, particularly on a broad scale, it can be understood as an outpouring. When believers respond in repentance and life transformation, it can be understood as a revival. When nonbelievers respond in great numbers, and masses of people across a broad geographical area are converted, it can be understood as an awakening.

When the Spirit is poured out, He operates at two levels. The first is in the revival of the church. Orr identifies three universal characteristics of genuine revivals: "an extraordinary burden of prayer, an unusual conviction of sin, [and] an uncanny sense of the presence of God." This then results in "repentance, confession, reconciliation, and restitution, with great concern for the salvation of sinners near at hand and far away."[3]

The second level is in the spiritual awakening of the populace. Not every revival produces an awakening, though we all wish they did. In the Book of Acts the initial outpouring of the Holy Spirit led to an instant reviving of the believers and an awakening of Jerusalem's populace. Three thousand came into the Church that day alone (2:41), after which more new believers kept coming, as "the Lord added to their number daily those who were being saved" (v. 47). Stephen didn't have it so well. Instead of receiving new converts, he was stoned and died as the Church's first martyr. But as the ensuing persecution scattered the Church, God used it to spread the awakening to Samaria and other regions.

The Holiness Revival and Holiness Movement

Is it accurate then for us to use the terms "Holiness revival" and "Holiness Movement"? Yes, on both counts. The Holiness revival was a revival because it transformed believers and churches. It brought many nonbelievers to salvation but was not quite broad enough to be commonly recognized as an awakening, though one might reasonably argue for it being so. The Holiness Movement was a movement because it got the momentum rolling beyond the revival to form churches, missions, and organized efforts that have gone on to propagate and nurture what the revival did.

Historically the Holiness Movement flourished a century ago in a tide of Holiness teaching and the formation of new organizations. But I would like to think it never died. Or better yet, I commit myself to doing my part in the rebirth or rejuvenation of the Holiness Movement. Would you join me?

To help us know where we're going, let's take a glance at revivals through the ages, then a closer look at the three essential and universal characteristics of genuine revival.

Revivals Through the Ages

The dramatic experience of Pentecost depicted in Acts 2 and the dynamic ministry of the church in Antioch (see Acts 11) were instances of the first outpourings of the Holy Spirit. Clearly the Holy Spirit was also poured out upon the persecuted churches of the Roman Empire, for they ultimately turned the empire upside down. From the 4th-century desert fathers to the medieval mystics, many individuals and groups experienced deep spiritual conviction and a heightened sense of God's presence. The extraordinary work of the Holy Spirit was present in the 12th-century persecuted renewal movement of the Waldensians. It appeared again in the 14th century with John Wycliff and his persecuted followers, the Lollards. The Holy Spirit surely worked behind Martin Luther and the Reformation of the 15th and 16th centuries, as well as the radical reformation Anabaptist movement, which was persecuted by the Reformers themselves. Spirit-led movements continued with the English Puritan reform of the 16th century and the 17th-century German Pietist renewal. The Spirit's outpouring propelled the 18th-century Moravians to unprecedented prayer and missions.

Revivals that resulted in general awakenings included the First Great Awakening, which in North America encompassed the late 1730s and the 1740s and continued to the 1790s in Great Britain, led by Jonathan Edwards, John Wesley, and George Whitefield; the Second Great Awakening, from the 1790s to 1840, led by camp meeting revivalists and Charles Finney; the Third Great Awakening, from 1857 to 1859, with D. L. Moody as a prominent evangelist; the Holiness revival, from the 1880s to the 1910s; and the worldwide revival, especially in Wales and Korea, along with Azusa Street, from 1904 to 1907. Numerous local revivals, renewals, and movements of the Holy Spirit have graced us since.

My own observations on the outpouring of the Spirit concur with those of Orr. We see that consistently through history outpourings result in the revival of the Church. In seeking to rediscover this work of the Holy Spirit, let us look at how Orr's three universal characteristics of revival have been exhibited in the past.

> During the weekdays of our revivals, we call for 6 A.M. prayer meetings. Most always these are surprisingly well-attended. During the Grove City, Ohio, Church of the Nazarene extended revival, 250 people, as well as their praise and worship team, would gather for the 6 A.M. prayer meeting.
>
> —E. P.

Extraordinary Burden to Pray

Before a revival ever hits, God plants in the hearts of intercessors an extraordinary burden to pray for revival. From them this motivation to pray spreads to others.

When revival hits, nonbelievers are also motivated to pray, but since they have no personal relationship with the Lord, their prayers naturally become those of repentance for salvation. This we will see in the section following. Believers are usually motivated to pray in one of several ways: for their own spiritual lives, for more outpouring of the Spirit, or for the salvation of nonbelievers. The Spirit of God commonly moves people to pray, but in times of revival, whole groups, whole congregations of people, are moved to intense prayer.

Morris Chalfant states that among those active in the Holiness Movement, the "outstanding characteristic above all others was that they were a people who prayed." He describes their "burden for souls": "They pleaded for anxious hearts. . . . They sought their own Gethsemanes. They appealed to God to give them the willingness to climb up their own little Calvaries. Sometimes they filled the night seasons with the longing cries for that holier interest in wayward and needy men."[4]

During a Nazarene camp meeting in Los Angeles in October 1898, the supernatural empowering of the Holy Spirit overwhelmed the people in a tidal wave of prayer and praise:

> As the people were engaged in prayer, there came upon them such a spirit of prayer that many began to pour out their hearts to God in all parts of the house, and there rolled over the assemblage such tides of glory and power that several lost their strength. Little was done during the rest of the service but to wait and praise, while such a sacred wave and heavenly glory filled the place as to be beyond all power of portrayal.[5]

Is your heart's desire to see more of this today?

Finney relates the fervency of a prayer meeting, where all the people were caught up in the Holy Spirit's inspiring presence and could do nothing but pray:

The brethren and sisters that were on their knees, began to groan, and sigh, and weep, and agonize in prayer. The deacon continued to struggle until he was about exhausted; and when he ceased my brother saith that there was nobody in the room that could get off from their knees. They could only weep and confess, and all melt down before the Lord. From this meeting the work of the Lord spread forth in every direction all over the town.[6]

With prayer meetings like this, it's no wonder they called upstate New York "the burned-over district."

Beginnings of the Third Great Awakening are traced in part to the famous "noonday prayer meetings" in New York City, which had a small beginning but astronomical increase.

Mr. J. C. Lamphier, a lay missionary in New York City, was greatly burdened for the salvation of souls. Almost daily in the lecture room of the old Dutch church on Fulton Street he would go alone to pray for a genuine revival. He finally decided to invite others to join him in prayer. He announced a weekly prayer meeting to be held at noon on Thursday, the 23rd of September 1857. . . . Before long the numbers increased and it became a daily prayer meeting. This meeting room overflowed, and simultaneous meetings were held in the other auditoriums of the church building. The seats were all filled, passages and entrances were blocked and hundreds were turned away for lack of room. This led to the formation of nine other daily noonday prayer meetings in New York City.[7]

Within six months 10,000 businessmen were gathering daily in New York City for prayer, and within two years a million converts had been added to the American churches.[8] Could this happen in your city?

In the early 1700s a group of Protestant refugees took refuge on the German estate of Nicolaus von Zinzendorf. Soon it was a thriving Christian community. With growth and diversity, pervasive

conflict arose. Then in August 1727 the Holy Spirit came powerfully upon the community. "On the Lord's Day, the tenth of August, their minister Rothe was seized . . . with an unusual impulse.
He threw himself before God, and the whole assembly prostrated
themselves with him under the same emotions."[9] A few days later
the people praised God, "hardly knowing whether they belonged to
earth or had already gone to heaven."[10] The Spirit's outpouring generated a prayer vigil in this Moravian community that continued
around the clock, seven days a week, and without interruption for
more than 100 years. You read that right, 100 years. Stop and imagine it.

Unusual Conviction of Sin

The Holy Spirit always convicts people of sin, leading unbelievers to faith and believers to a more genuine, purified Christian
life. In a revival the conviction of sin intensifies to extraordinary
proportions. People often experience a deep revulsion toward sin,
wanting to be completely free of it. Sometimes it happens with
dramatic, external manifestations; sometimes quietly and orderly.
The remarkable growth of the church in Africa was influenced by
the East African Revival of 1934 that continued for years and was
primarily marked by repentance and confession of sin.

Jonathan Edwards, the primary leader of the First Great Awakening, wrote of the movement of God in Massachusetts in 1740:
"There was scarcely a person in the town, either old or young, that
was left unconcerned about the great things of the eternal world.
. . . And the work of conversion was carried on in a most astonish-
ing manner, and increased more and more; souls did, as it were,
come by flocks to Jesus Christ."[11] As the awakening spread, a near-
by pastor reported that "more had been done in one week there
than in seven years before."[12] "Persons are first awakened with a
sense of their miserable condition by nature." With some, he said,
"their consciences are suddenly smitten," while "others have awak-

enings that come upon them more gradually."[13] However it may come, the Spirit's work makes all the difference.

John Wesley habitually dealt with people under severe conviction of sin as a result of God working through his preaching. Here is one example, typical of many: "A young woman followed me into the house, weeping bitterly, and crying out, 'I must have Christ; I will have Christ. Give me Christ, or else I die!' Two or three of us claimed the promise on her behalf. She was soon filled with joy unspeakable, and burst out, 'Oh let me die! Let me go to Him now! How can I bear to stop here any longer!'"[14]

A testimony of an early Nazarene believer tells both of conviction leading to conversion, followed by conviction and a long inner struggle leading to sanctification:

In October 1890, I was convicted of sin and soundly converted to God. In a revival meeting in Brooks, Iowa, the Blessed Spirit whispered, "Daughter, give me thy heart," and the devil whispered "Not to-night." The next day while at work in the kitchen, such a longing came into my heart to be saved that I fell on my knees and asked God in mercy to forgive my sins and make me His child. He answered my cry and took me into His arms. For several minutes I could only walk the floor exclaiming, "Precious Jesus, oh my precious Jesus!" and I promised then and there if He spared my life until the next night, I would go to the church and all in the house should know he had saved me. In August 1895, I was deeply convicted for holiness . . . but the things of the world held me back, and I went home with a heavy heart because I knew I was a disobedient child. I wanted Him to keep me, yet it was a hard struggle to keep faith alive. In June 1895, I came to California, seeking health and pleasure, and, with a friend, just *happened*, as it seemed, to visit the Church of the Nazarene. It was the last Wednesday night in September. I felt I had almost gotten into heaven as I sat there and listened to the prayers and songs and testimonies.[15]

Like people today, this person continued to struggle with her "in-bred evil nature" until being entirely sanctified a month later.

At a Holiness camp meeting in Texas under the leadership of C. B. Jernigan, the Holy Spirit brought dramatic conviction of sin. Jernigan read from Scripture and called for prayer. The Spirit moved his wife as she prayed. "Such a prayer as fell from the lips of Sister Jernigan was surely God-breathed. You could hear sobs all over the congregation." Then the song leader spontaneously sang. Finally Jernigan opened his message, saying, "The judgment was set, and the books were opened." At this point the Holy Spirit took over. Jernigan

> stood looking into the congregation in absolute silence for several minutes. Words were gone. He could think of nothing to say. You could have heard a pin drop during that time; the silence became painful, but still no one moved. In that great congregation of two thousand people some stood and some sat in perfect silence. Not a hand moved; not a sound was heard. All of a sudden a woman who had been professing holiness shrieked and fell from her chair into the straw, declaring that she was not ready for the judgment, and in just a few minutes people fell into the altar without a song, sermon, or a call, until there was no more room at the altar, and scores knelt at their seats praying at the very top of their voices. The scene beggars all description. Praying and shouting continued till far into the morning, and there were fifty-seven who testified to being saved in that one service.[16]

Does your heart not burn with desire for the work of God in your church? Who knows what could happen when we regularly give ourselves and our worship over to God?

In the worldwide revival of 1904-7 in Korea the Holy Spirit surprised two missionaries who had prayed for revival and were just going about their normal church ministry:

> While conducting the service in the usual way, many commenced weeping and confessing their sins. Mr. Swallen said he

had never met with anything so strange, and he announced a
hymn, hoping to check the wave of emotion which was sweeping over the audience. He tried several times, but in vain, and
in awe he realized that Another was managing that meeting;
and he got as far out of sight as possible. Next morning he and
Mr. Blair returned to the city rejoicing, and told how God had
come to the out-station.[17]

As conviction of sin increased, church people began repenting of
many things. This in turn opened the gates to an increased move of
the Spirit across the mission field, and conviction of sin intensified
yet more. In a subsequent meeting, "Conviction of sin swept the
audience. The service commenced at seven o'clock Sunday evening, and did not end until two o'clock Monday morning, yet during all that time dozens were standing weeping, awaiting their turn
to confess."[18] When people quit running for their cars after a worship service and instead stay to weep and confess, you know something good is happening.

Powerful Sense of the Presence of God

God is always with us through the presence of His Holy Spirit.
But to most of us most of the time, this is something we know by
faith more than by experience. In subtle ways through spiritual discernment, we sometimes gain an increased sense of God's presence
in our midst. In times of revival that presence is sometimes manifest in exceptional, sometimes dramatic, ways. Though hard to cat-
egorize, it is a sensation, sometimes tangible sometimes not, that af-
fects people's minds, emotions, wills, and occasionally bodies.

Wesley frequently experienced the manifest presence of God.
It was not anything he did, for he was not a sensationalist, he was
more likely to be stiff and solemn. Yet the Spirit moved mightily, as
he reported:

While I was enforcing these words, "Be still and know that
I am God," He began to make bare His arm, not in a closed

room, neither in private, but in the open air, and before more than two thousand witnesses. One, and another, and another was struck to the earth, exceedingly trembling at the presence of His power. Others cried with a loud and bitter cry, "What must we do to be saved?" And in less than an hour seven persons, wholly unknown to me till that time, were rejoicing, and singing, and with all their might giving thanks to the God of their salvation.[19]

Do you long to hear, "What must I do to be saved?" Would you be ready for those who fall to the floor under the power and conviction of God?

Edwards noted the presence of a powerful but invisible force influencing the minds of people all over New England during the First Great Awakening: "Many very stupid, senseless sinners, and persons of a vain mind, have been greatly awakened. There is a strange alteration almost all over New England among young people; by a powerful, invisible influence on their minds, they have been brought to forsake those things in a general way."[20] Contrasting Wesley's example, this power was not noticeable in itself, but it reaped a bumper crop of transformed lives. Always keep an eye on your radar screen for God's invisible power.

Grace Winona Woods says of the prayer meetings that initiated the revival of 1857-58, "The conviction was universal that this prayer revival was the work of God. . . . They were awed by the sense of Divine Presence in the prayer meetings and felt that this was holy ground. Christians were very much humbled. Impenitent men saw and felt this."[21] Ask for, and be ready to receive, God's divine presence in your meetings.

The powerful sense of God's presence goes beyond just a feeling, beyond people sensing it in their spirits. God's presence, when manifest powerfully, gets physical. One instance of this happened at an 1823 camp meeting near Liberty, Illinois, as recorded by one of the preachers: "Brother Harris fell back in the pulpit, overcome

CLEARWATER—Their classmates were probably snug inside their homes talking on their cell phones or e-mailing friends. But the high school students huddled in a semicircle near a small fire on Wednesday didn't care. . . . Members of their Christian teen group had something important to do for God, whom they consider the greatest friend of all. And it couldn't wait.

The group stood near the flames, which were fed by dozens of compact discs. Group members tossed them into the fire to prove their commitment to God during a revival at First Church of the Nazarene. . . .

Inspired by [the] final sermon of the revival, the group held an impromptu CD burning they considered an act of defiance against youthful, unprincipled modern-day life ruled by a risqué entertainment business.

Few staples of teen life were spared this ritual cleansing. Even a T-shirt that [one boy] doesn't believe represents Christian morals was burned. . . .

The high school students celebrated as the blaze melted the pile of modern-day materialism into unrecognizable sooty nothingness.

—*St. Petersburg Times*, "Revivals Still Kindle Christian Souls," January 17, 2004, 8.

by the influence of the Holy Spirit, and called upon me to invite the people forward for prayer. . . . The invitation was not sooner extended than the mourners came pouring forward in a body for prayer till the altar was filled with weeping penitents."[22]

The biggest meeting of the National Camp Meeting Association for the Promotion of Holiness was held at Manheim, Pennsylvania, in 1868. There the Holy Spirit swept across the congregation so powerfully that people felt what was like a strong wind. Nonbelievers were so scared by this that some stood "awe-stricken" and others ran away!

All at once, as sudden as if a flash of lightning from the heavens had fallen upon the people, one simultaneous burst of agony and then of glory was heard in all parts of the congregation; and for nearly an hour, the scene beggared all description. . . . Those seated far back in the audience declared that the sensation was as if a strong wind had moved from the stand over the congregation. Several intelligent people, in different parts of the congregation spoke of the same phenomenon. . . . Sinners stood awestricken, and others fled affrighted from the congregation.[23]

Do you dare to let God be Lord over your church meetings?

Often the power of the Spirit causes a person's energy to drain out or give way. This results in a kind of swooning (commonly called "being slain in the Spirit"), where one's physical body reacts to the powerful presence of the Holy Spirit and the person sinks flat on the floor. This is not a Pentecostal phenomenon. It seems to have happened in the Bible (1 Sam. 19:23-24; Acts 9:3-4). It happened among stiff Reformed churches under Edwards's ministry. It happened repeatedly with Wesley. It recurred all the way through the 19th century. And it has continued through the 20th century to today. A Methodist bishop writes of what happened at a conference in Gardiner, Maine, in 1825, while his colleague was preaching:

While he was preaching, the power of God rested upon the congregation and about the middle of his sermon it came down on him in such a manner that he sank down into my arms where I was sitting behind him just back of the pulpit. His silence focused every eye toward us. I instantly raised him up to his feet, and the congregation said his face beamed with glory. He shouted out the praise of God and it appeared like an electric shock in the congregation. Many fell to the floor like men slain in the field of battle. Hundreds were saved and family after family saw their children come to know the saving grace of Jesus in real personal experiences of new birth.[24]

Revivals are almost always marked by powerful preachers, though such preachers are usually as ordinary as any other preacher when there is no revival. The difference is that in revivals preaching and other ministries have a far greater effect.

Revivals are usually accompanied by church growth and sometimes by the emergence of new church organizations, such as the churches of the Holiness Movement. But church growth and the emergence of new churches are dependent on human leaders who go beyond enjoying the Spirit's blessing to evangelizing the lost and organizing churches to embrace new people.

One significant characteristic of revivals is that they have never been confined to one denomination or group. They may be limited geographically but never organizationally. The Holy Spirit has never shown any particular concern for distinctions between denominations. Eph. 4:4-6 affirms, "There is one body and one Spirit . . . one Lord, one faith, one baptism; one God and Father of all." The Holy Spirit comes when and where He chooses regardless of church boundaries.

FIRE-KINDLING QUESTION

What keeps you from travailing prayer, from pouring your heart out for more of God and for revival? What will you change in your life to be the person of prayer you can be?

3
DIFFERENCES IN REVIVALS
Amazing Variations of Revivals

"SHOUTING AND SINGING AND DANCING," "shaking," "cries of sinners," "a solemn awe," "a moving impulse to pray," "incurable diseases healed," "visions," "the abolition of slavery," "2,000,000 converts," "university colleges"—all of these and more have been visible
and very real occurrences during and in the wake of revivals
through the centuries.

While outpourings are always of the same Spirit (as we saw in
chapter 2), they and their subsequent revivals are often characterized with variety. Historical records of the reviving work of the
Holy Spirit testify to differing phenomena in different places, at
different times, and among different people.

Along with the universals of the extraordinary burden to pray,
conviction of sin, and sense of God's presence, some revivals and
awakenings exhibit certain visible phenomena, while others do not.
We first need to be aware that all these phenomena have occurred
in widely recognized revivals and awakenings. Their occurrences
have been historically validated. Second, we should be aware that
none of them are necessary to the Holy Spirit's work, since not one
of them has occurred every time. Thus we should not be fooled into insisting on any particular phenomenon.

The principle here is related to Jesus' patterns of healing
throughout the Gospels. Jesus was always the healer, and He always

On the night of the healing service at the 2000 Central Ohio District Camp Meeting, I anointed approximately 500 people. After that evening, I decided to pray silently over each person in subsequent healing services. I always instruct the crowd not to tell me their ailment, or even if they are praying in proxy for someone else. I remind them that Jesus has every hair on their head counted, and therefore, He knows what burden they are carrying on their heart. I further instruct them to silently pray in faith believing the Great Physician will hear and answer their plea. As a result, I have noticed a greater freedom to pray more specifically over each individual. Many miraculous healings have been testified to. A powerful, yet very sweet blanketing of the Holy Spirit, often referred to in services as a "holy hush," has also been observed. Most wonderful is that all attention is focused on God and not on any person.

—E. P.

healed those who cried out to Him. But He deliberately healed in completely different manners and methods. For example, He laid His hands on one person; He spit in the eye of another; He spit in the dirt and rubbed mud in the eye of someone else; for others He simply spoke. This was not by accident. Jesus knew humans well enough that if He did anything the same way more than a couple times, people would make a big deal out of the method. Before long they would inscribe in stone that "this is the way you must do it," all the while forgetting about the One who is actually doing it. Jesus radically varied His methods to force us to keep our attention on Him.

If you look through the Book of Acts, you will find the Holy Spirit working the same way. People spoke in other languages; then they prophesied; then they were put into a stupor as if drunk; then people were healed in strange ways; then earthquakes struck. But every time, the gospel was preached and lives were changed; nonbelievers got saved and believers got purified.

The same biblical pattern has held true throughout the continuing history of the Holy Spirit's work. Whether these differences are due to human responses to the Holy Spirit or different phenomena caused by the Spirit is difficult, if not impossible, to prove one way or another. Perhaps the fairest assessment is that on the one hand, the Holy Spirit manifests in power and instigates a human response, while on the other hand, different people react in different ways.

Here are the major human manifestations that occurred in response to past outpourings of the Holy Spirit.

BOISTEROUS MEETINGS

Outpourings of the Spirit naturally elicit human response. Thus it is no surprise that boisterous activity characterizes many revival meetings. The Holiness Movement exhibited this as sinners clamored to be saved in this service under Bresee in 1900: "The tide kept rising, and when the sermon was perhaps three-quarters through, there came such a cloud-burst of glory falling all over the congregation, that the preacher could not be heard, and he cleared the way for seekers to come to the altar. Before the meeting was over, there were three or four altar services in different parts of the church, and souls swept into the kingdom."[1]

Boisterous meetings also arose from the rejoicing of the saints, as observed in this Sunday service in 1898, also with Bresee:

The outpouring of the Spirit in the morning was so blessed that songs of praise and shouts of victory burst out in the midst of the preaching of the Word, in such a way as to make it at times impossible for Dr. Bresee to go on with his sermon.[2]

This was in a Nazarene church, just the way Bresee liked it. Boisterous meetings are often associated with the later Pentecostals, but the Holiness people had plenty of it first.

An 1800 revival in Red River, Kentucky, led by Presbyterians James McGready, William Hodges, and John Bankin, was one of those events that transformed the American frontier from lawlessness to godliness. But this Presbyterian meeting was not terribly orderly:

> William Hodges's sermon caused one woman to scream loudly, and before long, others were dropping to the floor, crying out, "what shall I do to be saved?" The official meeting came to a close and the three ministers left, but no one in the congregation moved. The McGee brothers had remained behind. Without warning, William McGee sank down to the floor, and John was trembling. He made one final appeal to the people to "let the Lord Omnipotent reign in their hearts and submit to Him." A woman shouted for mercy and John went to her side. Several people said to him, "You know these people. Presbyterians are much for order. They will not bear this confusion. Go back and be quiet." As a Methodist who perhaps did not wish to bring offense, he retreated and almost fell under the power of God. However, he returned, and "losing sight of the fear of man," he went through the place "shouting and exhorting with all possible ecstasy and energy." The floor was shortly "covered by the slain." According to McGready, the most notorious infidels were pricked to the heart, crying out, "what shall we do to be saved?"[3]

Any meeting can get boisterous if people get excited. The question is, what is the result? Does the fruit speak of the flesh or of God? Looking past these outward manifestations, we see that God was at work in people's hearts.

Shaking, Falling, and Crying Out

John Wesley experienced a fair amount of people shaking, falling down, and crying out in the crowds that heard him. For example, in Epworth, England, in 1742, he wrote: "And great indeed was the shaking among them: lamentation and great mourning were heard; God bowing their hearts so that on every side, as with one accord, they lift up their voice and wept aloud."[4] The following day he recorded: "While I was speaking, several dropped down as dead, and among the rest such a cry was heard of sinners groaning for the righteousness of faith as almost drowned my voice. But many of these soon lifted up their heads with joy, and broke out into thanksgiving, being assured they now had the desire of their soul—the forgiveness of their sins."[5] In fact by the later years of his ministry, Wesley had experienced so much of this that he grew tired of it and wondered if it were the devil causing such "extravagance."[6] Actually this is possible. When demonic spirits are subject to the powerful presence of God, shaking, falling, and crying out are sometimes manifestations of the demonically afflicted. I have seen this in my ministry. We all see this repeatedly in the Gospels when demonized people cry out, fall, and writhe at Jesus' feet (see Mark 1:21-28; 5:1-20; 9:17-29). But this is not to say that every falling or crying out is a demonic reaction to God's power. People under deep conviction of sin and agony of soul may do the same.

The early 19th-century camp meetings often witnessed uproarious gatherings. Moses Hoge described the Cane Ridge, Kentucky, camp meeting in 1801:

> The careless fall down, cry out, tremble, and not infrequently are affected with convulsive twitchings. . . . Sinners dropping down on every hand, shrieking, groan-

Jen Boen had attended church for over 30 years yet never knew Jesus as her personal Savior. On March 18, 2002, she attended the Danville Southside Church of the Nazarene's revival and was gloriously saved! An excerpt from her testimony:

"Ever since I was saved March 18, 2002, I have been completely and radically changed. I have lost all desire to sin, and I am able to recognize sin immediately. . . . After visiting Grandma's I know how much this is all true. I am no longer the Jen they knew."

—*Jen Boen. Letter to E. P., March 28, 2003.*

ing, crying for mercy, convulsed; professors praying, agonizing, fainting, falling down in distress, for sinners or in raptures of joy! . . . As to the work in general there can be no question but it is of God. The subjects of it, for the most part, are deeply wounded for their sins and can give a clear and rational account of their conversion.[7]

Important here is that though the outward manifestations got noticed, the leaders gave their attention to what was happening in the hearts of the people. People received salvation, and their lives were transformed. That's what counts.

SILENCE

Sometimes the presence of God brings an awe-filled silence, akin to what is expressed in Hab. 2:20: "The LORD is in his holy temple; let all the earth be silent before him."

Often the Holy Spirit's presence was so strong in Wesley's ministry that a hush fell on the crowd. At Newcastle on December 12, 1742, the congregation did not stir. Wesley wrote, "When the sermon was done, they divided to the right and left, none offering to go till I was past; and then they walked quietly and silently away, lest Satan should catch the seed out of their hearts."[8] Have you ever been in that silent hush of the Spirit?

Years later Wesley wrote again in Wellington, England, "The church was moderately filled in the morning; in the afternoon it was crowded in every corner, and a solemn awe fell on the whole congregation while I pressed that important question, 'What is a man profited if he should gain the whole world, and lose his own soul?'"[9]

An observation of a camp meeting at Des Plaines, Illinois, in the 1860s found that "silence was a wonderful power with them; the vast assembly awaiting on God, just waiting. . . . Not a word said, but every heart opened heavenward, and God pouring his blessing in. The results in bringing souls to Christ estimating no other good that was done, marks the meeting a signal success."[10] Be encouraged when you see Christians sitting in silence. God may be at work on their souls.

NORMALITY

Since meetings where nothing outwardly unusual occurs are not big news items, we do not get many reports about how modestly people behaved. But lots of people, maybe most, never react in any demonstrative, external way. Yet the Holy Spirit does His work within them.

The 1857-59 revival was distinctive for having few of the ordinary manifestations. Keith Hardman agrees with others in saying, "What impressed observers, and the press, was that there was no fanaticism, hysteria, or objectionable behavior, only a moving impulse to pray."[11] Interestingly, when the same revival spread to India, many "signs and wonders, tongues and strange actions occurred, unlike the revival in the United States." Orr considers these miracles and strange behaviors to have been necessary to authenticate the revival among people in those lands, whereas "in the U.S. people were receptive."[12]

Finney, used to all manner of manifestations during his ministry, commented on a revival in Stephentown, New York, "The meetings were uniformly characterized by perfect order, and great solemnity. The[r]e were no indications of wildness, extravagance, heresy, fanaticism or of anything deplorable."[13]

Most revival meetings have been characterized by orderliness (not to be confused with stiffness or solemnity) rather than pandemonium. The First Great Awakening, with leading figures Edwards, Wesley, and Whitefield; the 19th-century camp meetings; and the Azusa Street Revival were frequently marked by outward manifestations. Most other revivals, at least in North America, have been more outwardly ordinary.

HEALINGS

Physical healings in revivals have been reported throughout the centuries, including during the 1857-59 revival and the Holiness Movement. Chalfant reports that in Holiness revivals "incurable diseases were healed; broken limbs were straightened; blind eyes were opened; tuberculosis, typhoid fever, pneumonia—all manner of diseases were healed."[14] Pentecostals have also reported many physical healings from the beginning of their movement.

The early Church of God (Anderson) leader and founder, Daniel Warner, made physical healing and other miracles a regular part of his itinerant ministry. "Marvelous healings accompanied their ministry, and time and again Warner boldly prayed God to stop the rain that might hinder a service. There were a number of instances where his prayers were answered and the rain held off till the worshipers returned home."[15]

Emotional healing, that is, recovery from past emotional and psychological pain, is harder to pinpoint, since it is nonphysical and less likely to be quantified and documented. But the abundance of testimonies of people's changed lives strongly suggests that emotional healing was very common among participants in the revivals.

CHARISMATIC PHENOMENA

Charismatic phenomena, particularly the practice of glossolalia, have historically been the most controversial. The Pentecostal Movement, rising out of the worldwide 1904-7 revival, suddenly made "speaking in tongues" the initial mandatory sign for the infilling of the Holy Spirit. But these "tongues" were not actual languages like those of Acts 2. Originally leaders in the Holiness Movement showed little reaction to this. But the Pentecostals doggedly insisted that a person practice their reduced form of glossolalia to be considered baptized in the Holy Spirit. This rang hollow to Holiness leaders and to countless thousands who had already experienced the anointing power of the Holy Spirit during the previous 25 years of the Holiness Revival. This Pentecostal insistence led to divisions that have persisted to this day.[16]

The very same revival that gave us Azusa Street and the Pentecostal Movement hit Wales and Korea first in 1904, making an even greater impact in those countries than it did in the United States. But this is the curious fact: "During the Welsh Revival, there occurred charismatic phenomena, uncanny discernment, visions, trances but no glossolalia." The same is true in Korea; in fact the Presbyterian and Methodist churches were so dynamic that when the first Pentecostals arrived there after World War II, people felt no need for them.[17]

Nevertheless, charismatic phenomena have occurred since then in some places, though not in others, where the Holy Spirit has been poured out.

Dreams and Visions

Supernatural dreams and visions occasionally appear in revival times. At a revival meeting in Oakland in 1889 under Maria Woodworth, an elderly man came to observe:

> As he looked over the congregation, he made some light remark to his friends about the display of the power of God, and started boldly up towards the pulpit to investigate, but before he reached the pulpit he was struck to the floor by the power of God and lay there over two hours. While [he was] in this condition, God gave him a vision of hell and heaven, and told him to make his choice of the two places. He called upon the Lord to save him and said he would choose Christ and heaven.[18]

At a Holiness revival in east Texas in 1898, led by the widely beloved Bud Robinson, we see another example:

> While Rev. Bud Robinson was in charge, a young man fell into a trance on Monday and lay in this condition for forty-eight hours. He was seen by hundreds of people and examined

by many physicians while in this unconscious state. He stuttered until he could scarcely be understood before this, but when he came out of the trance, he preached to the great crowds that thronged him for more than an hour, without stuttering one time. He told of his visit to both heaven and hell while in this condition. He told of meeting many people who had long ago died in the neighborhood; some he met in heaven, others in hell.[19]

Dreams or visions like this, which are common in the Bible, should not be accepted uncritically or rejected uncritically but be assessed by their harmony with Scripture and their positive spiritual impact. The first one led to the man's salvation. The next one brought physical healing and a rousing testimony of heaven and hell. How would you interpret the visions?

In the Hebrides Islands in 1949 church leaders, under the leadership of Duncan Campbell, pleaded with God for months, house by house whole communities were drawn to prayer. When revival first hit, people felt objects as well as themselves physically shaking. They reported visible, supernatural lights hovering over many of the farmhouses. Donald John Smith remembers, "There were lights coming on houses. The glory of the Lord was shining round about." Around 4 A.M. hundreds of people gathered from surrounding areas, mysteriously drawn "by an incomprehensible power." People were even lying down on the road, crying out to God to have mercy on them. Churches overflowed.[20] We see how all kinds of phenomena might occur when God comes near in power.

Wesley dealt very much with these supernatural experiences as well. He offers wise advice to us in how to respond to them and assess their validity:

What I have to say touching visions or dreams is this: I know several persons in whom this great change was wrought in a dream, or during a strong representation to the eye of their mind, of Christ either on the cross, or in glory. This is the fact;

let any judge of it as they please. And that such a change was then wrought appears not from their shedding tears only, or falling into fits, or crying out: these are not the fruits as you seem to suppose, whereby I judge, but from the whole tenor of their life.[21]

This is the basic premise for Christian experience in general. Experiences themselves are secondary. How they affect the whole tenor of our lives and relationship with God is primary.

MUSIC

All of our Wesleyan hymns were born in revival. Fanny Crosby's hymns were revival hymns. Go ahead and look them up. See how many you know. Check the dates. Even "Jesus Loves Me, This I Know" came from the 1857-59 revival.

Take a look at any hymnal and you will find that a preponderance of hymns, especially the joyous, victorious hymns, and those that speak of our sin and Jesus' sacrifice on the Cross were written during one of the three great awakenings.

SOCIAL REFORM

In the First Great Awakening, Jonathan Edwards was amazed and delighted at the habits people quit because of the transforming power of the Holy Spirit. Nothing had worked to make them change, until the presence of God caused them to quit

their frolicking, vain company-keeping, night-walking, their mirth and jollity, their impure language and lewd songs. . . . And there is a great alteration amongst old and young as to drinking, tavern haunting, profane speaking, and extravagance in apparel. Many notoriously vicious persons have been reformed and become externally quite new creatures.[22]

If the government harnessed the power of God, it would lower our taxes! Government services could be cut in half.

It was the Second Great Awakening that tamed the westward

migrating settlers. Kentucky and Tennessee were known as lawless places. The evangelist Peter Cartwright described southwest Kentucky: "Here many refugees from almost all parts of the Union fled to escape justice or punishment. . . . It was a desperate state of society. Murderers, horse-thieves, highway robbers, and counterfeiters fled there, until they combined and actually formed a majority."[23] The Holy Spirit did in these places what no government was able to do. For decades across the expanding frontier, lawlessness was overcome by holiness.

A prosecuting attorney in Rochester, New York, examined local population and crime statistics after the 1830 revival led by Finney. He stood amazed at the revival's effect, saying,

> "I have been examining the records of the criminal courts, and I find this striking fact, that whereas our city has increased since that revival threefold, there is not one third as many prosecutions for crime as there had been up to that time.

> "Thus crime," he says, "has decreased two thirds, and the population has increased two thirds. This is," he said, "the wonderful influence that that revival had had upon the community."[24]

You can fetch your calculator and figure out the statistical impact of revival.

Nowhere has the social impact of revival been more dramatic than in the 1904-7 Welsh revival, led by Evan Roberts. One British reporter wrote: "It is sweeping over hundreds of hamlets and cities, emptying saloons, theaters, and dance-halls, and filling the churches night after night with praying multitudes. The policemen are almost idle; in many cases the magistrates have few trials on hand; debts are being paid; and the character of entire communities is being transformed almost in a day."[25]

The Welsh revival even produced a slowdown in the coal mines. Because the foulmouthed miners got converted and cleaned up their language, the horses no longer understood what they said!

It took time for the horses to learn the new language before they started hauling properly again. A manager reported, "The horses are terribly puzzled . . . The haulers are some of the very lowest. They have driven their horses by obscenity and kicks. Now they can hardly persuade the horses to start working, because there is no obscenity and no kicks."[26] Does the need for social reform where you live motivate you to pray?

Other significant reforms include the Abolition Movement that rose out of the Second Great Awakening and helped abolish the slave trade. Movements for prison reform; child labor laws; women's rights; and care for the blind, deaf, sick, aged, and mentally ill also emerged from revivals.

MISSIONS

The Moravians, who maintained a round-the-clock prayer vigil for 100 years, did not stop there. Their amazing passion for prayer translated into a passion for missions, which became the dominant characteristic of the Moravian movement. For over 28 years this group of refugees sent missionaries to 28 countries—that is easily more than all the other Protestants combined had sent out in the previous 200 years.

The British and Foreign Bible Society, as well as the American Board of Foreign Missions, the very first American mission agency, both grew out of the Second Great Awakening. Many others followed. The Third Great Awakening spawned Hudson Taylor's China Inland Mission, the very first of the interdenominational faith missions. The Student Volunteer Movement for Foreign Missions, founded in 1888, rose out of the impetus of revival and the personal ministry of D. L. Moody and others. It stands as one of the greatest missionary movements ever and bore as its motto "The evangelization of the world in this generation." In that generation more than 20,000 students went to world mission fields before the movement declined under rising swamps of the same liberalism that Holiness churches have stood against.[27] What new mission advances do you think could surge out of a revival today?

CHURCH GROWTH AND NEW ORGANIZATIONS

Every major revival and awakening has brought tremendous church growth. The church around the world would be nowhere near what it is today were it not for the mighty forward surges it took as a result of outpourings of the Holy Spirit.

In the Second Great Awakening, Methodists grew from 1,500 members in 1784 to just under 1 million in 1830. Baptists doubled between 1802 and 1812. Presbyterians grew from 18,000 in 1807 to nearly a quarter million in 1835. This growth could not have been due to immigration, since the British interfered with European migration to North America during the Napoleonic wars until 1815.[28] Growth was by conversion, especially during revival.

In the Third Great Awakening, Orr calculates that "numerically, the 1858 Awakening added approximately 2,000,000 converts to the various churches, and the available testimony suggests that the quality of the conversions was excellent and abiding." Here is the contingency associated with the churches that grew more: "Denominationally, every evangelical church fellowship gained from the 1858 Revival. Their gains were proportionate to their evangelical-evangelistic strength, and inversely proportionate to the strength of anti-evangelical traditions among them."[29]

"Between 1893 and 1900, twenty-three new denominations rose out of the Holiness Movement in America."[30] The original Church of the Nazarene organized in 1895 with 135 charter members. Ten years and many new churches later the movement counted 3,195 members, of which 1,500 belonged to the original church.[31] And this was before the church merged with the Association of Pentecostal Churches of America in 1907 and the Holiness Church of Christ in 1908.

EDUCATION

The First Great Awakening made a big impact on education, starting with the promotion of education for pastors. "Nine university colleges were established in the Colonies during the thirty years following 1740, and six of them directly or indirectly sprang from the Awakening: Brown, Columbia, Dartmouth, Pennsylvania, Princeton, and Rutgers. The first five presidents of Princeton were outstanding evangelists."[32]

Great moves of the Holy Spirit normally generate the means and institutions for training new godly leaders.

FIRE-KINDLING QUESTION

Think back on all the outward things that might occur in revival. What might you do to open yourself more to what the Holy Spirit might surprisingly do in your life?

4

A BIBLICAL VIEW
Scripture's Call to Seek the Spirit

THE TERM "REVIVAL" DOES NOT APPEAR IN SCRIPTURE. But references to the conditions and phenomena of revival abound. The phrase "outpouring" or "pouring out" of the Holy Spirit appears repeatedly, because God is pleased to lavish us with His Spirit. Prayers for the Spirit's outpouring and promises and stories of it also fill the Bible, because people have always hungered for God.

Scripture exhorts us to continually seek and draw near to God. Repenting and humbling ourselves are the surest ways to do this. God's presence through His Spirit may be subtle and ongoing or abundant and overwhelming.

In the Old Testament we find many accounts of spiritual renewal where Israel establishes or reaffirms covenants with God. Spiritual and covenantal renewal occur under Moses; during the reigns of David, Solomon, Asa, Jehoshaphat, Hezekiah, and Josiah; and also under Elijah, Zerubbabel, Haggai, Zechariah, Ezra, and Nehemiah. But these renewals rarely lasted, and Israel's spiritual temperature perpetually oscillated up and down.

Throughout the Old Testament we find the Spirit of God being poured out. But not until the New Testament do we see His Spirit dwelling within people. Only after Jesus ascended and the Church received "the gift of the Holy Spirit" (Acts 2:38) did the Spirit take up residence in people. This is why Old Testament revivals never had the enduring impact that those in New Testament times and later had.

In the New Testament the Holy Spirit dwells in each believer. His presence is a "deposit guaranteeing our inheritance" (Eph. 1:14) and a "deposit, guaranteeing what is to come" (2 Cor. 1:22). Our "inheritance" and "what is to come" refer primarily to our promise of heaven. But now we live "between the times." We follow Jesus in this age of "already but not yet."[1] We live between the time of already having fellowship with God through Jesus Christ but not yet having immediate fellowship with God in heaven. In salvation we have the Spirit's "seal of ownership on us" (2 Cor. 1:22). We also have the baptism with and continual filling of the Spirit (Matt. 3:11; Eph. 5:18). Here's the wonderful part: however much God has given us His Spirit, we haven't seen everything yet. God has more for those who hunger.

Second Cor. 1:20 affirms that "no matter how many promises God has made, they are 'Yes' in Christ." This text, written before the New Testament was compiled, means that every promise in the Old Testament is valid for those who are in relationship with Christ. The same verse concludes, "And so through him the 'Amen' is spoken by us to the glory of God." "Amen" is a term of sincere agreement meaning "truly," "indeed," or "may it be so." This all means that every biblical promise of God's Spirit is valid for Christians today, and our part is to sincerely agree with that promise.

The New Testament was written to churches during the time of the Holy Spirit's initial outpouring. This outpouring caused a great awakening. We may even call it "The Original Awakening." Churches were popping up everywhere in the Roman world as a result of that initial outpouring. Because these churches already had the Holy Spirit in abundance, we do not find many New Testament promises that God would pour out the Holy Spirit or cause revival. God does not need to promise people things they already have.

But since the church has repeatedly swayed to and from God over the last 2,000 years, we continue to need His Spirit's outpouring! Let's take a look at God's promises and exhortations surrounding this outpouring.

TURNING FROM GOD AND TO GOD

God laments in Jer. 2:13: "My people have committed two sins: They have forsaken me, the spring of living water, and have dug their own cisterns, broken cisterns that cannot hold water." This is the continual sin of humanity. People turn away from God, and then they presume they can find life, truth, and fulfillment without Him. But they can't. None of us has what it takes. And even if we did, we would leak! The daily busyness, pressures, and troubles of daily life tend to drain our living water. When believers or churches are dry, it's a good sign they have drifted away from God's "living-water spring." If we don't drift toward sin, we drift toward a busy, programmed life.

God reaches out to us in 2 Chron. 7:14: "If my people, who are called by my name, will humble themselves and pray and seek my face and turn from their wicked ways, then will I hear from heaven and will forgive their sin and will heal their land." You've probably heard this preached, prayed, and maybe even sung. We are *His* people. He *desires* to share His Spirit with us. But we must (1) humble ourselves—too few people do, and pride is the church's (and humanity's) most pervasive sin; (2) pray—this is the only way to move in the spiritual realm and is best done continually and fervently; (3) seek His face—that is, seek His very presence, not just what He gives us; and (4) turn from our wicked ways—wickedness is anything, even good things, contrary to God. His promise is to hear us, forgive our sin, and heal our land. How our land needs healing! We have seen in the first three chapters of this book how the outpouring of the Holy Spirit heals the land.

The most critical part of turning to God is repentance. It is the one word that sums up the above paragraph on 2 Chron. 7:14. "Repent!" was the first word out of the mouth of John the Baptist as he preached (Matt. 3:2). It was the first word out of Jesus' mouth when He began to preach (4:17). It was at the core of Peter's preaching (Acts 2:38; 3:19), and we see it woven through all of Paul's letters to the churches. Repentance does not mean to feel sorry. God shows little interest in how we merely feel. The New Testament uses two words for repentance: *metanoeo* means "to have a change of heart"; *epistrepho* means "to turn around," "make an about-face." God expects this of unbelievers so they can express a genuine faith and enter a relationship with Him. And He expects it of believers so they can experience His promised fullness of the Spirit. In the letters to the seven churches, in Rev. 2—3, all but two churches were told to repent. The church in Smyrna lived under persecution and poverty, which will surely cleanse a church. And the church in Philadelphia, although weak and under oppression, endured faithfully. The rest were told to repent of forsaking their first love of Jesus, tolerating bad teaching, tolerating sin, being spiritually asleep, and being lukewarm. Most churches, especially in wealthy, politically free nations, will find a place on that list. Churches, even Holiness churches, must repent before those outside them will.

The other side of repentance is found in the examples of Nehemiah and Daniel, what I call "intercessory repentance." In Dan. 9, Daniel identifies himself with the sins of Israel during the Exile and repents at great length on their behalf. This does not bring the Israelites any personal forgiveness (for that, each one must repent separately), but God did respond personally and powerfully to Daniel, not only with an end-times prophecy but also by moving King Cyrus's heart to let the Israelites return to Jerusalem. In Neh. 1:4-11, at the end of the Exile, Nehemiah identifies himself with the sins of Israel and confesses on their behalf. Again this does not bring the Israelites any personal forgiveness, but it does open the way for Nehemiah to return to Jerusalem and rebuild the walls. The basic principle is this: Though each person must personally repent to receive personal forgiveness, when a leader or intercessor repents on behalf of his or her followers, it seems to open the way in the spiritual realm for God to operate.

You may be in a family or church situation that needs your intercessory repentance. You yourself may simply need to repent. Isn't it worth the blessing of God?

THIRSTING FOR GOD

Absorb into the depth of your heart this cry from the depths of David's heart while he was in the desert fleeing King Saul's assault:

> O God, you are my God,
> 　earnestly I seek you;
> my soul thirsts for you,
> 　my body longs for you,
> in a dry and weary land
> 　where there is no water.
> I have seen you in the sanctuary
> 　and beheld your power and your glory.
> Because your love is better than life,
> 　my lips will glorify you.
> I will praise you as long as I live,
> 　and in your name I will lift up my hands.
> My soul will be satisfied as with the richest of foods;
> 　with singing lips my mouth will praise you.
>
> *(Ps. 63:1-5)*

His thirst, or we often say hunger, is earnest. In the midst of dryness his thirst is so compelling that he feels it physically. Have you craved the presence of God so much you actually felt it physically? Those who passionately desire the supernatural presence of God in their lives often feel a physical sensation in that longing. The good news is that David doesn't experience longing alone. He experiences God's supernatural presence in its power and glory. He knows very personally the love of God, and he praises God for it. He is satisfied.

Later David hungers again and spreads out his hands (the biblical posture for prayer) in this powerful image of Ps. 143:6: "I spread out my hands to you; my soul thirsts for you like a parched land." You have surely seen ground so dried up it formed mazes of cracks and fissures. If that ground could speak, it would cry out for water, loudly and desperately. If David had maintained that thirst, he might never have fallen with Bathsheba. How would a deep, gripping thirst or hunger for God change your life? How would it change your church? Without it you will never pray persistently for the blessings of the Spirit, because you'll give up. With it you will be spiritually alive, connected with God, and experiencing His Spirit—with or without an outpouring.

These scriptures remind us never to be content with only studying God's Word. The Pharisees did that. We must also absorb it and live it to where it becomes a description of our lives.

GIVING OF THE SPIRIT

God again uses the image of dry ground when He promises in Isa. 44:3-5 to pour out His Spirit:

> For I will pour water on the thirsty land,
>> and streams on the dry ground;
> I will pour out my Spirit on your offspring,
>> and my blessing on your descendants.
> They will spring up like grass in a meadow,
>> like poplar trees by flowing streams.
> One will say, "I belong to the LORD";
>> another will call himself by the name of Jacob;
> still another will write on his hand, "The LORD's,"
>> and will take the name Israel.

Are we dry, thirsty land? I hope so! The Lord promises here to pour out His Spirit on the descendants of Israel. Remember: Every promise of God is "'Yes' in Christ." Long for it. Seek it. Expect it. The last half of this passage expresses the new identity people will have in response to the Spirit's outpouring. It happens in every revival. People's lives are transformed, and they gain a new sense of identity as children of God.

God reiterates the importance of humility and repentance in Isa. 57:15:

> I live in a high and holy place,
>> but also with him who is contrite and lowly in spirit,
> to revive the spirit of the lowly
>> and to revive the heart of the contrite.

A "contrite" person is one who is ready to repent and grieve over sin. A "lowly" person is humble. A genuinely holy person is all of these. Thankfully we don't have to be oppressed to receive this promise; we can be "poor in spirit" as Jesus says in Matt. 5:3 (KJV). Keep in mind that God makes His home in two places: in heaven and in the hearts of those who are humble and contrite. His promise, twice, is to revive such people. Remember this if you want to be revived!

Joel 2:28 prophesies that "afterward, I will pour out my Spirit on all people." He promises that prophecies, dreams, and visions will be given. This outpouring will come upon both men and women. And this pouring out of the Spirit will coincide even with supernatural signs and wonders in heaven and on earth. In the initial outpouring of the Spirit of Acts 2, Peter quotes Joel 2:28-32, applying it to New Testament times. In fact, since we are still between the times of "already" and "not yet," this prophecy of Joel, like many prophecies, has more than one chronological application. Joel's promise of the Spirit's outpouring applied to Acts 2. It also applied to the revivals and awakenings of the 18th through 20th centuries. And with the fearful signs and wonders yet unfulfilled, expect it to apply to the coming end-times.

Every year during the Feast of Tabernacles, the high priest poured a vessel of water taken from the Pool of Siloam over the Temple altar and prayed for continued rain and blessing. Jesus knew our greater need was for spiritual refreshing. And it may have been at this time that Jesus stood in the midst of the great crowd and raised His voice declaring a promise of the Holy Spirit:

> "If anyone is thirsty, let him come to me and drink. Whoever believes in me, as the Scripture has said, streams of living water will flow from within him." By this he meant the Spirit, whom those who believed in him were later to receive. Up to that time the Spirit had not been given, since Jesus had not yet been glorified *(John 7:37-39)*.

Like King David, Jesus calls people who are spiritually thirsty. What He is promising here is not so much the Spirit's outpouring but the Spirit's abundant abiding within a believer. This is the residual blessing of those who seek God's face. Even if God does not send revival, He still provides a personal abundance of the Holy Spirit in our lives.

In Acts 3:19, where we earlier saw Peter urging his hearers to "repent" *(metanoeo)* and "turn to God" *(epistrepho)*, he also tells them why: "so that your sins may be wiped out, that times of refreshing may come from the Lord." His phrase "times of refreshing" is the closest the New Testament comes to using the term "revival." Peter was speaking to people who had not yet received Jesus as Lord and was offering them the hope of the Spirit's fullness. Yet as we have seen, since New Testament times, the Church has continued to need such "times of refreshing." May the Spirit pour out again even today!

OLD TESTAMENT REVIVALISTIC EXPERIENCES

Three revivalistic experiences stand out in their fervency and effect on the people. These experiences under Hezekiah, Josiah, and Ezra resemble the revivals of the past two centuries. Yet they also exhibit how different the Old Testament position with God was from ours.

Hezekiah began his reign by purifying the Temple of the idolatry of the previous two kings. Second Chron. 29—31 describes this revivalistic experience. Hezekiah restored sacrificial offerings and worship, then called the people throughout Judah and most of Israel to return to the Lord. For those who responded, this call to turn from wickedness and serve the Lord resulted in abundant and prolonged praise and celebration. In the description of this experience (30:26—31:1), we see two important elements of revival—a burden to pray and the presence of God:

> There was great joy in Jerusalem, for since the days of Solomon son of David king of Israel there had been nothing like this in Jerusalem. The priests and the Levites stood to bless the people, and God heard them, for their prayer reached heaven, his holy dwelling place. When all this had ended, the Israelites who were there went out to the towns of Judah, smashed the sacred stones and cut down the Asherah poles. They destroyed the high places and the altars throughout Judah and Benjamin and in Ephraim and Manasseh.

This powerful encounter with God resulted in dramatic spiritual renewal and the destruction of ungodly worship practices across the country. Yet even after this and more, Hezekiah's son, Manasseh, "did evil in the eyes of the LORD" (33:2). Almost unbelievably he restored all the pagan practices that his father had tried to get rid of.

We read in 2 Chron. 34—35 that from his youth, King Josiah began to purge Israel of the spiritual waywardness resulting from the half-century reign of Manasseh. In the process the high priest discovered the Book of the Law (what we know as the books of Moses, the Torah). When the secretary read it, Josiah tore his robes in grief and repentance for what Israel had done. The prophetess Huldah prophesied to him, telling him that because he humbled himself and repented, the Lord heard him. Josiah renewed the Mosaic covenant, and the people pledged themselves to it (34:29-32). He then removed idols, articles for Baal and Asherah worship, high places, pagan altars across Israel, and even killed the pagan priests. After this Josiah celebrated a Passover unlike any "since the days of the prophet Samuel" (35:18).

Although not an outright revival, this was certainly a renewal in which the Holy Spirit was active. We see here one of the important elements of revival—the conviction and confession of sin. In this case Josiah repented on behalf of the people, and the people agreed to turn back to the Lord. We also see radical reform (frequent in revivals) that changed the entire spiritual state of the nation. Unfortunately, and to us amazingly, none of this seems to have passed on to his son, Jehoahaz, who succeeded him. Jehoahaz and every king that followed him "did evil in the eyes of the LORD." The Babylonian invasions came, and then it was all over until the end of the Exile (see 2 Kings 23:31—25:30).

This, as well as Manasseh's lapse into idolatry, is a graphic illustration of what so often happened throughout the Old Testament because God had not yet privileged people with the personal indwelling of His Spirit. Please! Do not take the Holy Spirit's indwelling lightly. Before Pentecost the Spirit was external—except in rare cases and for rare purposes, and at that it was temporary.[2] We see the results of this—not only individuals but the whole nation would flip-flop almost immediately from faithfulness to idolatry.

After the return of the exiles, Neh. 8—10 records how Ezra recognized this ongoing problem of renewal and relapse. Though the people did not have the indwelling presence of the Holy Spirit, Ezra knew they did have the Law. Unlike the people's behavior, the Law was constant. So "he read it aloud from daybreak till noon." As he did, "all the people listened attentively" (8:3) and "lifted their hands and responded, 'Amen! Amen!' Then they bowed down and worshiped the LORD with their faces to the ground" (v. 6). After uproariously celebrating the Feast of Tabernacles,

> the Israelites gathered together, fasting and wearing sackcloth
> and having dust on their heads. . . . They stood in their places

and confessed their sins and the wickedness of their fathers. They stood where they were and read from the Book of the Law of the LORD their God for a quarter of the day, and spent another quarter in confession and in worshiping the LORD their God *(9:1-3)*.

This passage shows us two revivalistic elements—the confession of sin and the powerful sense of the presence of God.

Aware of the people's tendency to lapse, Ezra tried to go beyond just smashing idols. Chapter 10 tells in detail how he made a binding agreement with the people, even putting it in writing and having the priests and Levites affix their seals. Today, although we have the indwelling of the Spirit, many people still revert to their old ways. Binding agreements with God might be something you or your church might seriously consider.

THE HOLY SPIRIT'S NEW TESTAMENT MINISTRY

The Holy Spirit powerfully anointed John the Baptist in his ministry of leading people to repentance in anticipation of the coming of the Messiah. He was clear, though, that it would be Jesus who would baptize people with the Holy Spirit.

Jesus had the fullness of the Holy Spirit every moment of every day. Power flowed out of Him to others through touch and spoken word. The Spirit was His Spirit and was manifest in His healings, miracles, and the powerful impact of His teachings. He promises in John 14—16 that we will do even greater things (most of us are still working on that) and that the Spirit will comfort us, guide us into all truth, teach us all things, and make known to us the things of Jesus. In Luke 11 Jesus gives His most concentrated exhortation and promise on prayer and receiving the Holy Spirit: To receive we must pray with persistent boldness (v. 8). When we continually ask, seek, and knock, we will receive (vv. 9-10). When we ask for the Holy Spirit, our Father in heaven will give Him (v. 13). By faith let's ask God in prayer to fulfill His Word in us!

In 1974 at the age of 20, God radically saved me. Before then, I never knew about Jesus. Although my salvation was a genuine transformation, my Christian walk was up and down for the next 13 years. . . . In 1987, after growing dissatisfied with my walk, I sought God for more. In a desperate wrestling match of sorts, God revealed to me the carnality, pride, self-sufficiency, and rebellion of my heart.

Eventually, I surrendered everything to Him. In exchange, God sanctified me wholly! He cleansed my heart and filled me with the Holy Spirit! It has been nearly 20 years, and I have never been the same! Glory to His holy name!

—E. P.

The outpouring of the Holy Spirit at Pentecost and the original awakening that followed were all about evangelism. People spoke languages they did not know as a demonstration that the gospel was for all people. Later, persecution forcibly scattered them as missionaries. People were so overcome by the Spirit that outsiders thought they were drunk. The Spirit then brought prophecy to all the Church; no longer was it reserved for officially recognized prophets. The Spirit caused earthquakes when people prayed, both in a prison and in a prayer meeting. Most important, the Spirit radically changed people's lives. The Spirit's outpouring generated repentant new believers and new churches everywhere. Lives were transformed from the top of society to the bottom until the world's great superpower, the Roman Empire, turned upside down. For the first time, the Spirit was for everyone.

Accordingly, every believer was given spiritual gifts and expected to bear the fruit of the Spirit. Every believer was exhorted to have intimacy with God and be filled with the Spirit. No longer only a generic, communal experience the tribes of Israel shared, the presence and work of the Holy Spirit was now a personal, life-transforming encounter.

As in every outpouring, some believers went to excess, thinking and behaving in fleshly ways in response to what the Spirit was doing. Paul saw through this, especially in his letters to the Corinthians, and distinguished the genuine work of the Spirit from the unacceptable behavior of people. He neither accepted fleshly behavior nor hindered the work of the Spirit. This is an important principle for us to learn today. We'll look more closely at this in chapter 6.

PRESENCE OF GOD—COMMON AND OVERPOWERING

Every believer has the indwelling of the Spirit as part of the new birth. Similarly, the Body of Christ as a whole experiences the "common" presence of God; that is, we know by faith, and sometimes by experience, that God is always present with us. Jesus said, "I am with you always" (Matt. 28:20). Every believer also has the opportunity to be filled with the Spirit. Just as the Body of Christ as a whole may experience the overwhelming presence of God, as we see it in revivals. God has indeed promised, "I will pour out my Spirit."

Throughout the Old Testament those who wanted to be in God's presence had to go to whatever place God chose to be. That place was always at the center of the community. Before the tabernacle was constructed, Moses set up "the tent of meeting," where he met God face-to-face (Exod. 33:7-11).[3] The overpowering presence of God was at that time given only to Moses. The people greatly honored this and worshiped God whenever the cloud came down and Moses entered the tent. Moses hungered intensely for the presence of God. He asked to see God's face, but God mercifully would show him only His "back," saying, "no one may see me and live" (v. 20). Such is the overwhelming glory of God. When Moses came down the mountain after receiving the Ten Commandments for the second time, "his face was radiant because he had spoken with the LORD" (34:29). The people were so fearful of this supernatural glow that He kept His face veiled.

Throughout the wilderness wanderings, God's presence was

In January 2003, my family flew to Pasadena, California, to hold a "Prayer Awakening" seminar for the Los Angeles District, as well as revival services at Pasadena First Church of the Nazarene.

Midway through a morning session, we stopped for a short break. I was sitting on the first row waiting for the others to return, when the glory of the Lord fell on me! All I could do was weep. No words would form, only tears. . . . I humbly asked God to "take care of the service. . . ."

Finally I returned to the pulpit. The entire time I was praying . . . , the altars had been filled over and over again. . . .

Pastor Jay Ahlemann later announced: "Sunday evening through Wednesday evenings . . . the altars were lined that night and each succeeding night. Many showed up for 6 A.M. prayer meetings. According to [86-year-old] staff pastor Willis Gray, 'This was the most powerful revival witnessed at First Church of the Nazarene in Pasadena since the 1940s.'"

—E. P.

embodied in the pillar of cloud and fire that constantly hovered above the Tabernacle. The entire community regularly experienced this "common" presence of God through the provisions of manna and incidents of judgment, healing, and blessing. When the cloud moved, the people moved: "Whenever the cloud lifted from above the Tent, the Israelites set out; wherever the cloud settled, the Israelites encamped" (Num. 9:17). Aren't you glad you don't have to pick up and move just to be with God?

After settling in the Promised Land, the Temple became the place where people regularly went to pray and hold festivals in the presence of God, and still today the Western Wall of the Temple's foundations is the holiest site of Judaism. But when the Temple was first dedicated, it "was filled with a cloud, and the priests could not perform their service because of the cloud, for the glory of the LORD filled the temple of God" (2 Chron. 5:13-14). When the glory of God shows up, things are *not* business as usual.

This same glory shook Isaiah in the Temple (Isa. 6:1-8) and overwhelmed Daniel in a vision

(Dan. 10:7-8). Although the 12 disciples experienced the "common" daily presence of Jesus, they and others also witnessed astounding miracles. Three of them were overwhelmed at the Transfiguration (Matt. 17:1-8). The glory prostrated Saul, who became Paul (see Acts 9:3-4). It filled the Early Church at Pentecost (chap. 2) and at prayer (4:23-31).

God's "common" presence today is always with us. But the record is clear—He occasionally blesses us with His overwhelming presence as well.

FIRE-KINDLING QUESTION

Which passage of Scripture most motivates you to hunger more for God and earnestly seek Him? Underline and bookmark that passage in your Bible. Refer to it daily, memorize it, and share it with God. Watch what happens in your life.

5
WHAT ARE WE LOOKING FOR?
How to Expect and Not Expect Revival

No two revivals have ever been the same. Keep that in mind when you ask God for revival. Local settings, types of people, and historical circumstances seem to affect how the Spirit's outpouring is received and expressed.

People "hold revivals" or, more recently, "do revivals." If you can "hold" or "do" a revival, it's not a revival. Holding a revival would be like holding a hurricane! It cannot be planned, programmed, or contained. Only God sends revivals. We may hold an evangelistic campaign, spiritual life conference, or any kind of "let's commit ourselves to God" meeting. These important meetings are vital to a healthy church's annual calendar. But by definition they are not revival. "Revivalistic meeting" would be a more accurate term. It denotes a meeting where we are truly seeking revival, while honestly acknowledging that we cannot program one.

What Are We Really Hoping For?

When we say we want revival, what are we really hoping for? Way too much assuming goes on here. Do we hope for God to show up and do anything He wants? Judging by history, many people might not be prepared for that and would be scared if He did.

Do we hope for a meeting where lots of people go to the altar, sign cards, and use lots of tissue? That's a common one (and generally my favorite).

Do we hope for a meeting where pandemonium breaks out? Some do. (Despite the messiness, it might be good exercise. In fact the historical anecdotes we've seen suggest that early Holiness people often got their exercise at church. Pentecostals only got more exercise and added new sounds.)

Do we hope for a meeting where everything is respectable, not too much happens, and we can still vaguely say, "God blessed"? Too many of us settle for that.

I think it's safe to say that if we ask God to pour himself out on us, we can trust Him if and when He does. In any case what we *hope for* will influence what we *do* to prepare for it. So let's be careful what we hope for.

"HOW TO HAVE A REVIVAL"

Charles Finney originated or developed many of the practices associated with revivalistic meetings that are still in use today: the altar call, mobilizing people for home visitation, and scheduling special nightly meetings in church buildings that sometimes last for weeks. He seemed to focus less on God's will and more on human choice and technique as the key for revival. He even stated, "A revival is the result of the *right* use of the appropriate means." It just needs "the blessing of God." A revival, he said, "is as naturally a result of the use of the appropriate means as a crop is of the use of its appropriate means."[1] This means that if you do the right thing in the right way, and God blesses it, you get a revival. Methods thus became important. The problem was that people who followed him often sought techniques rather than the Holy Spirit. They adopted Finney's methods and implemented them effectively, calling such meetings "revivals." Calling revivalistic meetings "revivals" thus went hand in hand with using methods that presumably would bring on a revival. And it still goes on today.

Book titles such as *How to Promote and Conduct a Successful Revival* (Revell, 1901) and *How to Have a Revival* (Sword of the Lord, 1946) testify to the human tendency to reduce spiritual things to methods.

To have a successful meeting we are elsewhere told to "set the date early," "secure evangelistic help," "plan adequate publicity," "locate prospects," and properly use the information through meetings and committees.[2] We are also told that for a successful meeting, we must pay attention to "type and timing," "preparation," "prayer," "recruitment," "music," "prerevival preaching," "buildings and property," "altar workers," "printed material," "follow-up," "finance," "entertaining God's man," "correspondence," "the perfect setup," and "developing a revival mentality."[3] A successful revival meeting, we are told, also includes a "revival council," a "prayer committee," an "attendance and enlistment committee," a "program and altar workers committee," and a "follow-through and Bible study committee."[4]

Actually these guys are largely right. Programmatic details are part of successful meetings (though some of us would rather skip the committees). But where is the focus? Before we tangle with details, we must determine what our activity is all about. Otherwise we risk exhausting our energy and resources on human efforts to get God to do something. We must answer this key question: Is our objective to promote successful meetings, or is it to seek a genuine moving or outpouring of the Holy Spirit? If you take this question seriously and frequently remind yourself of it, it will pay back enormous long-term benefits.

In all the above lists, the *only* item that relates to the essence of genuine revival is prayer. Historical accounts of genuine revival put little or no emphasis on any of the other items on the lists. While these "how to" approaches help us organize our programs, our attention is far too easily drawn to the approaches themselves. Why? Because humans inherently go after programs. Programs make us feel that we are doing something, and they're easier than developing deep spirituality.

Unfortunately, approaches and programs can demand so much of our attention that we have little left over to give to seeking God. You cannot serve two masters. One will invariably dominate. And through most of the 20th century, programs have won out. Focusing on the mechanics of revivalistic meetings has actually hindered revival. Think about that.

Clearly, mechanics do not convince the Holy Spirit to pour himself out. It would be great if all we had to do was put a good program together and *voilà!* Revival. But God knows us humans. If He had set things up that way, we would be constantly manipulating the Holy Spirit's activity. If we really think about it, we can be thankful God does not work that way. Remember the Scripture: If anything leads to an outpouring, it is repentant, hungry hearts travailing in prayer (Isa. 66:1-3; Ps. 63:1-5; Luke 11:5-13).

Lawrence Hicks, whose story we opened with in chapter 1, tells it better than anyone else:

> I have often observed that widespread advertising, as essential as good advertising is, will not bring the desired crowds to our evangelistic efforts. I have sadly noted so very few new faces in our revival meetings. I have been greatly discouraged over the lack of new material to feed the mills of our altars. I have seen the "old straw" threshed and rethreshed until it is worn threadbare. I have tried this method and that, this program and that, in my human zeal and earnest endeavor to "have a revival"—only to see the sheer mockery of failure! Yet I know the need. I am aware of the solution. Hindrances face us all, everywhere. These hindrances are too great and too powerful and too manifold for mere humanity or wit to overcome. We must have something from beyond the ordinary walks of men. We must have the supernatural. We must have God! He comes only in the operation of the Holy Ghost.[5]

He goes on to emphasize, "Once a great Holy Ghost revival sweeps into a congregation one sees the foolishness of much of the costly effort that we humans expend."[6]

What does Hicks seek instead? Basically what we have seen in chapters 1 and 2: "Sinners will fall under deep conviction. Christians will feel the distinct rebuke of the Spirit for any laxness and looseness in devotions, ethics, and daily walk. A consequent return to the fundamentals of the faith will be felt by all concerned. The sanctifying of believers, the restoration of backsliders, the humbling of the holy, will all be seen and felt to be part of the revival."[7] We need programs and mechanics of revival to manage and channel the work of the Spirit for optimal long-term results. But we must remember that programs and mechanics never did and never will cause a genuine revival to occur.

T. M. Anderson, a leading evangelist of the Holiness Movement, said, "Unless the preachers and people in the holiness movement take time to pray and give less time to programs and plans, the movement will soon be in woeful want of spiritual power to withstand the evils of the modern age."[8] He said this nearly a hundred years ago! How much more applicable it is today. I have attended too many meetings, including denominational pastors' meetings, where far too little time is given to prayer. Is it any surprise that churches across our land, including Holiness churches, are rich in programs but poor in the "spiritual power to withstand the evils of the modern age"?

Finney: Fiction and Fact

The truth about Finney's effectiveness in revivals, which he never fully acknowledged, had little to do with his methods. His style was attractive, and his methods effective, but I contend that these were not what brought the Holy Spirit's conviction upon thousands of people.

The effectiveness of his revivals lay with the man behind the scenes of the revivals—a man whom few people saw and whom

Finney talked astonishingly little about. Few people on this planet have ever prayed with such endless, prevailing fervor as Daniel Nash, Finney's intercessor. We have no existing photo or any kind of drawing or depiction of Nash. Until recently, no books were ever written about him. He was a pastor for six years, during which he experienced two revivals. After being treated badly by his congregation, he joined Finney and went into towns ahead of Finney to pray. He recruited others to pray with him, and he often prayed for three or four weeks before the meetings started. He prayed through the duration of every meeting, and rarely showing his face, he fasted and travailed in prayer all day long.[9] God's response to this devotion is what generated the spiritual power behind the great stories about Finney as an incredible evangelist. His greatest and most famous ministry happened in Rochester, New York, in 1830-31, and as usual Nash prepared the way and prayed fervently the entire time.

This is how important Nash was to Finney. Within four months after Nash's death in December 1831, Finney withdrew from full-time evangelism, and in September 1832, he took a pastorate in New York City. He later became a professor and then president of Oberlin College. The revival lasted in the northeastern United States until the mid 1840s. But during this time Finney's evangelism was less frequent and more likely to be done in areas where the Spirit was already working.

This granddaddy of revival methods admitted at length in his college magazine, *The Oberlin Evangelist*, in 1845 that converts were not sticking to the Christian faith as they had in 1830-31.[10] Learn the lesson here! Methods may attract people, but they do not attract the Holy Spirit. Methods may get some people to confess their sins, but they do not produce genuine converts who stay with their faith. Only the Holy Spirit can do that. He did it then, and He still does it now through prayer.

TRUE REVIVAL WILL TAKE YOU
BEYOND CHURCH BOUNDARIES

Locally, revival will take you into your neighborhood or city or network of family and friends. When Jesus is vibrantly alive in your heart, you feel compelled to share Him with someone else. New power infuses evangelism and ministry, reaping abundant results.

Broadly, revival will take you beyond denominational lines to mix with like-minded people who may be in other organizations. This was the nature of the Holiness Movement. It crossed all denominational lines. If we want the Holiness message to continue spreading, we must continually take it across denominational lines.

Because denominations did not change in response to the Spirit's work during the Holiness Movement, new Holiness denominations emerged. Hopefully these same Holiness denominations will continue responding to genuine moves of the Spirit that may sweep our land today. Just as it was during the Holiness Movement, if church leaders today resist the Holy Spirit, many of their people will follow Him to where He is welcomed. Let's make sure we welcome Him in the church we attend!

Reviving works of the Spirit may shake up programs and power structures of local churches. They may also shake up programs and power structures of denominations. This can be threatening to some. Yet if the Lord is behind the shake-up, we'd be wise to say, "Yes, Lord." Pray that those affected would have a greater desire for the Lord's work than for their own activities and would rise to ever-higher levels of Spirit-filled ministry. I want to see our denominations and organizations infused with new life and power. Don't you? Isn't that what all denominationally affiliated people claim they want?

God has never sent a revival limited to a denomination. Every revival and awakening in history has spilled over denominational lines to whoever received it. Jesus said, "I, when I am lifted up from the earth, will draw all men to myself" (John 12:33).

GIVE ME THAT "OLD-TIME RELIGION"

Past revivals often used the terms "old-time religion" and "old-fashioned revival." To modern ears this may induce thoughts of worn-out traditionalism. This is not the case.

From the late 1800s modernism elevated science and rationalism to almost divine status, exalting evolution as its primary idol. Across the country the tide of modernism introduced churches to higher criticism, which ingloriously dissected Scripture like a lab specimen. Skeptical attitudes arose toward miracles and the Lordship of Christ. Spiritual lethargy spread across the church—as it still does today. William McLoughlin describes the challenge of modernism at that time:

> The loss of confidence in divine support of old beliefs and values mounted from year to year. . . . Darwinism, which had seemed a remote and abstract theory when *The Origin of Species* appeared in 1859, now loomed up in every book, sermon, periodical, and tract to challenge the most fundamental tenets of the old faith. It challenged the Bible by denying its account of creation. It challenged the concept of an absolute moral law by its doctrine of survival of the fittest. It challenged the millennial goal by describing nature as amoral and purposeless.[11]

Timothy Smith observes that after 1910 a nationwide controversy between fundamentalism (at that time meaning an adherence to the fundamentals of the Christian faith) and modernism inundated churches. "It intensified greatly all the issues dividing rural and urban America, and drew a sharp line between men who sought new religious horizons and those who clung to the old-time faith."[12]

"Old-time religion" was essentially shorthand for a biblically orthodox faith that accepted the truth of Scripture and acknowledged the Lordship of Christ. "Old-fashioned revival" likewise meant a wholehearted response to the outpouring of the Holy

Spirit. From 1929 to 1933 Los Angeles First Church of the Nazarene printed at the top of its Sunday bulletin: "The Church of the Old-time Religion." From 1934 to 1936 the bulletin read: "A Church with the Old Gospel for the New Age."

In 1899 the *Nazarene Messenger* printed a favorite chorus:

> *'Tis the old time religion,*
> > *That's done so much for me;*
> *'Tis the old time religion,*
> > *That sets my spirit free;*
> *'Tis the old time religion,*
> > *Gives glory in my soul;*
> *'Tis the old time religion,*
> > *That cleansed and made me whole.*[13]

The style is outdated, but look at it again and you'll see that the content is the same as what we believe, seek, and practice today. Though we now see their style of doing things as old-fashioned, style had nothing to do with it. It was entirely an issue of biblical faith, just as it is now. So, yes, today even the most contemporary and cutting-edge churches practice "old-time religion" and seek "old-fashioned revival."

RECENT 20TH-CENTURY MOVES OF THE SPIRIT

Though this book mainly refers to Holiness revivals of the 18th and 19th centuries, the Holy Spirit has been working all along, and in ways too broad to cover in one volume. That said, it may help our overall grasp of where we've come from and where we're going to briefly mention the three broad, defining Christian movements in the latter half of the 20th century: the Evangelicals, the charismatic renewal, and the third wave.

Evangelical faith, by definition, has been around since the time of Jesus. Modernism paved the way for liberal teachings on Scripture in the church. Liberalism, along with a tolerance of sin, was what the Holiness Movement stood against, and those not in Holiness and other Bible-believing churches were susceptible to it. Many in North America thought liberalism would continue to rise until Bible believers died out. But two world wars and the work of the Spirit led many people back to the Bible. The aftermath of World War II witnessed a surge of belief in the Bible as the true Word of God and the necessity of spiritual rebirth as a qualification for being a true Christian.

Evangelicals distinguished themselves from the more narrow fundamentalists by turning away from sectarianism, cultural isolation, and anti-intellectualism. They articulated a fresh, confident gospel message and engaged themselves culturally and intellectually with the surrounding society. The most prominent figure in this rise of evangelicalism was Billy Graham. The phenomenon of mass evangelistic crusades and the dramatic rise of evangelical churches, educational institutions, parachurch organizations, and mission agencies was surely a broad work of the Holy Spirit.

In 1960, Dennis Bennett, rector of St. Mark's Episcopal Church in Van Nuys, California, and many in his congregation began having charismatic experiences. After many years and controversies, the charismatic movement has not become a church or denomination; rather it has pervaded many denominations as a renewal movement and has spawned many independent churches. Unlike the Pentecostal movement, it does not define any kind of "prayer language" as the sign of the baptism in the Spirit. It gives more attention to the diversity of spiritual gifts.

Disagreement may arise as to the Holy Spirit's role in the charismatic movement, but whatever the true nature of the movement and its attending experiences, countless people have testified to a renewal of their faith. It has deeply affected many in the Roman Catholic Church as well. Its influence has waned and given way to the most recent movement.

"The third wave" is a term coined by C. Peter Wagner in the early 1980s. The first and second "waves" were the Holiness/Pentecostal and charismatic movements respectively. As the next in line, the "third wave" expresses the resurgence of the Holy Spirit's work in the 1980s until now. It is thoroughly evangelical and evangelistic. And it is distinguished by its subtlety—a calm, gentle work of the Spirit. The Holy Spirit has revitalized churches around the world with little or none of the controversy that has attended the Pentecostal and charismatic movements. This is because those aware of this work of the Spirit do not demand a particular experience from anyone and are very open and interdenominational in thinking and practice. Many churches renewed in this move of the Spirit are not even aware of its identity.

In the third wave laypeople are equipped for doing ministry. Spiritual gifts are practiced and encouraged, but no single gift is considered essential. Emphasis on prayer has been a primary mark, and prayer meetings and prayer movements have risen up all over the globe in recent years. Much of the surge of new Christian worship music since the 1980s is also part of this work of the Spirit. Its impact is perhaps broader than anything else that has come upon the church worldwide. It has touched denominations and believers in almost every place. Holiness churches everywhere have been among those experiencing third wave renewal.

DO PEOPLE HAVE DESIRE?

I pray for the outpouring of the Holy Spirit all the time. I often join other people in prayer for the outpouring of the Spirit and for revival. Yet my day, like yours, gets busy or distracted. If I'm not careful, I get lackadaisical in my prayer. I must deliberately remind myself that my need for God is greater than my need for anything else in the day. This often leads me to the simple prayer, "Lord, increase my hunger for You!" It works! As I begin to pray, the desire for God begins to flow into a river of hungry prayer.

This is a problem of human nature again. Most of us have to be

> To travail in prayer can be hard work. It takes time. It takes discipline. It takes determination. I believe E. M. Bounds describes it well: "It may be said with emphasis that no lazy saint prays. But to really pray, to pray until hell feels the ponderous stroke, to pray until the iron gates of difficulty are opened, to pray until the mountains of obstacles are removed, this is hard work, but it is God's work and man's best labor."
>
> —*E. M. Bounds*, E. M. Bounds on Prayer. *New Kensington, Pa.: Whitaker House, 1997, 63.*

hard pressed before we'll passionately pursue something the way the persistent widow pursued the judge in Jesus' parable of Luke 18. She didn't allow that judge a day of rest. "Persistent boldness" is the fullest translation of the word Jesus used in the parable of the obnoxious friend at midnight in Luke 11:8 to describe how He wants us to pray. At the end of the persistent widow episode Jesus essentially asks whether He will find, when He comes, people with that sort of persistent and bold faith, the kind that seeks Him without giving up. Will He? Will you be one?

It's not easy when you have small children or a demanding work schedule. You may go through seasons in your life when God leads you to pour your heart out in travailing prayer. You may go through seasons in your life when you need to get through other demands and simply cannot pray as much as you'd like. Yet just as seasons never last forever, so also we must not put off our God-ordained call to seek Him and the pouring out of His Spirit.

If you would seriously pray for revival, you must commit hours of time. Prayer for the Spirit's outpouring is not a prayer of convenience. It is a prayer of sacrificial commitment, because to do it you will invariably have to sacrifice other things. To do that you must have more desire for God than for all other things.

Longing Generates More Desire than Having

My high school friend Paul was in love with Roslyn. She was a beautiful cheerleader and honor student. She was demure, reserved, refined, and kind. Roslyn was a high-class, wonderful human being in every way we could figure. Paul was not looking for any carnal conquest. He just longed for the privilege of taking her on a respectable date. He burned with a passionate desire to have the honor of her presence for an evening.

Finally he got his courage up and asked her. And . . . she said yes! Ecstasy.

The day after I couldn't wait to ask my questions. How did it feel? Will she go out again? What's the chance of going steady? I finally saw him and blurted, "Well? How was it?"

"It was OK."

"OK? You were near death in your longing for her. She accepted your invitation. And it was just *OK*? What's wrong with you!"

Paul furrowed his eyebrows and mused. Finally he concluded, "I guess when I finally got my date with her, I didn't really want her so much anymore."

"You're nuts!" I spouted. I did not even have the guts to ask out a beauty like her.

The issue with Paul I later discovered is the issue with most humans most of the time. We want that toy, that car, that house, that job, that potential relationship so badly. Then we get it. We eventually get used to it. Then we take it for granted, and we feel, "So what?"

I see this universal axiom at work everywhere: Longing generates more desire than having.

This, I believe, is a reason why God does not lavish himself on us more. God knows us. He knows the behavior of our hearts. So He sometimes withholds himself to encourage us to hunger more for Him. This first draws us nearer to Him, because it keeps us coming. Second, it makes us more like Jesus, because longing generates

Christlikeness. He wants us to long for Him, to love Him above all else. He wants us to be like Jesus above all else. Withholding himself draws us closer to Him, because it generates desire in us.

BROKEN VESSELS

If you go before God, seeking an outpouring of His Spirit, remember one thing: God uses broken vessels. A vessel is a container for holding something. Most of us spend way too much energy trying to look good. But Ps. 51:17 says, "The sacrifices of God are a broken spirit; a broken and contrite heart, O God, you will not despise." I don't mean broken in the defeated sense but in the godly sense. Godly brokenness happens when the things that would hinder our union with God are broken. Godly brokenness happens when love for God transcends everything in the world (the essence of holiness). Godly brokenness happens when Isa. 66:2 describes us: "This is the one I esteem: he who is humble and contrite in spirit, and trembles at my word."

Godly brokenness can come from trouble, as when hardships cause someone to be humbled and open to God. Or it can come from God, as when He moves our hearts to be humbled and open to Him. Godly brokenness says "Yes, Lord" and turns every pain or humility into a bridge to drawing closer to God. I know that I was of little use to God until I accepted godly brokenness in my life.

> True humility is not found in hanging our heads declaring our unworthiness. To Jesus we are worth more than all of the kingdoms of the world. Genuine humility is a constant, radical dependence on God.
>
> —E. P.

When we seek a response from God, we need to be broken from pride (especially spiritual pride), greed, laziness, anger, sexual lust, envy, backbiting, fear, addictions, and anything that hinders our union with God. We also need to be broken from the mentality of self-sufficiency. This is not just an overt decision but also an unexamined presumption that we can do things on our own power to get God to respond—and even if He doesn't, we'll put together a good program so something happens anyway. The more we empty ourselves and walk in humility (godly brokenness), the more response God promises us and the less we're tempted to resort to programs.

FASTING

Fasting is a central practice for broken-vessel people of prayer, since it both expresses and results in brokenness before God. Fasting is a physical way of praying and humbling ourselves before God and saying to Him, "I'm serious about this!" It brings about a brokenness before God that comes in no other way. Thus fasting is often a key to spiritual breakthrough.

Isaiah 58 tells us the attitude God looks for in our fasting. The "fasting I have chosen," says God, purposes to free others from injustice, oppression, hunger, and lack of clothing and shelter. The fasting of God's choice has nothing to do with self-centered piety. It's all about "Thy Kingdom come, Thy will be done." These are among the very things that happen because of revivals! When we fast and pray in this way, Isa. 58:8-9 promises that our "light will break forth"; our "healing will quickly appear"; and God's righteousness and glory will surround us. That's revival!

If you are not used to fasting, start where you are able and go from there. For most of us that's one meal a day. Although you must allow for any personal health concerns, fasting is actually good for the body. Your body cleans itself out when you fast. The Lord will also clean your soul when you fast.

The Bible does not command fasting but strongly encourages it, even depicting three ways of doing it. In a "dry fast" you do not eat or drink anything at all. This is what Moses and Jesus did supernaturally for 40 days. In a "total fast" you do not eat anything, but you do drink liquids. This seems to be the most common kind of fast in the Bible, and it's the most common kind of fasting done to-day. People generally drink water but also fruit or vegetable juices. You can fast one meal a day, a whole day, several days, or longer. In a "partial fast" you abstain from certain types of food, for example meat, fine foods, beverages other than water, desserts, sweets, and snacks. This is also called a "Daniel fast," after Daniel's practice in Dan. 9:2-3. God honors all three types.

Fasting is not a place for legalism. Strictly speaking, fasting is refraining from eating, not to lose weight, but to intensify a person's seeking of God. Broadly speaking, we can see fasting as the voluntary denial of a normal function for the sake of intensified spiritual activity. This means you can fast anything. The idea is to give sacrificial focus to God, where you might otherwise indulge yourself or give your attention to something else. Fasting is feasting on God. Start where you're at and go from there.[14] God knows your heart.

No Revival? You've Still Got Renewal!

If you don't experience the outpouring you pray for, don't go beating yourself up! As much as God expects you to pray, the work of His Spirit is up to Him, not you. In the big picture, you can actually be thankful for that. Better to live in the tension of having spiritual hunger yet meekly submitting to God than to hunger and get upset if you don't get what you requested.

Even if you don't experience revival, you can still undergo spiritual renewal. In fact, renewal is a byproduct of seeking revival. Try it. Consistently seeking revival naturally renews you!

Remember Jesus' promise in John 7:37-38: "If anyone is thirsty, let him come to me and drink. Whoever believes in me, as the Scripture has said, streams of living water will flow from within him." This, says the next verse, is the Holy Spirit. While a revival comes like a flood, renewal comes in streams. Many factors influence whether and how a revival comes. But renewal does not seem to be as dependent on external factors as revival. Believers with hungry hearts are readily renewed, as are congregations who consistently seek the Lord.

Unlike floods, which occur only occasionally, streams flow all the time. They are not as impressive, but they flow continually. And, just like revival floods, they are wet. Spiritual renewal can be, and should be, an ongoing habit of every church and individual! Keep your hunger and renewal flowing; enough streams of renewal can easily result in a flood.

In my church we experience spiritual renewal all the time. To us it's an expectation. We expect ourselves to hunger for God, and we expect God to answer according to the promises of His Word. As a congregation our spiritual renewal becomes an ongoing lifestyle that breeds joy and unity. Any healthy, Spirit-filled congregation will experience the same.

In this kind of setting, individuals regularly experience the types of things characteristic of revivals. That is, when Christian communities seek and practice renewal as a normal experience, individuals frequently experience conviction of sin, an extraordinary burden to pray, and a strong sense of God's presence. They also experience things described in chapter 3. The only difference is that masses of people don't experience them at the same time as they do in full-blown revival. But here and there they do experience them.

The consolation prize of having renewal but not revival is that it is easier to manage (as we will see in the next chapter) and more likely to be a protracted, long-term experience.

A Balancing Attitude

Here's an attitude that will keep you in balance. It has a broad scriptural foundation, pleases God, and balances the emotions of a believer's heart between contentment and desire. The attitude is this: Be thankful for what you have, but hunger for more.

FIRE-KINDLING QUESTION

When you seek revival or renewal, what exactly are you seeking? What price will you pay for either one? Think about these things and commit to them before the Lord.

6

PRESENT EXPERIENCE AND ETERNAL SPIRIT
How to Handle Revival

THE HOLY SPIRIT IS ETERNALLY THE SAME, but people are different. Those differences show up in human needs, cultures, personalities, and responses to the Spirit (or what people think is the Spirit). How do we avoid mixing these things up?

HISTORICAL RESPONSES TO REVIVAL

Though you cannot "hold" a revival, you can manage one. In fact, if you get one, you had better manage it, or a blessing could breed problems. Great leaders of revivals through history have wisely distinguished the work of the eternal Spirit from other experiences of people. They did so by focusing attention, not on outward things, but on what God was doing in people's hearts.

The work of the Holy Spirit needs leaders who neither indiscriminately accept everything that happens nor stop things out of hand. When church leaders of the past embraced everything that happened, chaos sometimes ensued, with more attention given to theatrics than to changed hearts. When church leaders opposed the work of the Spirit, the group experiencing revival invariably moved out, and the opposing group experienced little or none of the Spirit's work.

Accordingly, from the time of the First Great Awakening, people have inclined toward one of three positions in times of revival:

those who oppose anything unusual; those who tend toward the excessive; and those who maintain critical open-mindedness and steer between the two extremes. Rather than doing a whole chapter on this, let us look to Jonathan Edwards's principle and John Wesley's example.

Edwards, the earliest and greatest theologian of revival, was the first champion of the middle course and set the standard for all wise leaders and participants in revival. He wrote voluminous observations on revival and biblical interpretations of what was going on. For example: "Whatever imprudences there have been . . . and whatever error in judgment, and indiscreet zeal; and whatever outcries, and faintings, and agitations of the body, yet it is manifest and notorious that there has been of late a very uncommon influence upon the minds of a very great part of the inhabitants of New England." He goes on to list the evidence of this influence: "seriousness" about "the eternal world"; a "great disposition to hear the word of God preached"; and people changed from being "vain, thoughtless persons" to being "serious and considerate" and having a "vast increase of concern for the salvation of the precious soul."[1] Edwards was quite accepting of all sorts of behavior, as long as he could discern that the Spirit of God was centrally operating.

Wesley encountered all manner of reactions to his preaching. He writes of a rather humorous case in Wapping, England, in 1739, where one woman was offended by the manifestations, then got quite a surprise.

Many of those that heard began to call upon God with strong cries and tears. Some sunk down, and there remained no strength in them; others exceedingly trembled and quaked; some were torn with a kind of convulsive motion in every part of their bodies, and that so violently that often four or five persons could not hold one of them. I have seen many hysterical and many epileptic fits; but none of them were like these in many respects. I immediately prayed that God would not suffer those who were weak to be offended. But one woman was offended greatly, being sure they might help it if they would—no one should persuade her to the contrary; and was got three or four yards when she also dropped down, in as violent an agony as the rest. Twenty-six of those who had been thus affected . . . promised to call upon me the next day.[2]

Any preacher would welcome such a finale!

When considering outward manifestations and the inward work of God, Wesley offers this humble and open-minded assessment we all should heed: "Perhaps it might be because of the hardness of our hearts, unready to receive anything unless we see it with our eyes and hear it with our ears, that God, in tender condescension to our weakness, suffered so many outward signs of the very time when He wrought this inward change to be continually seen and heard among us."[3] In other words, God uses outward signs to overcome the hardness of our hearts.

Then again, Wesley also wisely does not give too much credence to outward manifestations. When it comes to manifestations versus substance, he imparts the pithy statement "Blossoms are not fruit."[4]

Throughout revival history, the responses that have saved people from missing out or overindulging and have kept the work of the Spirit going forward have followed the lead of Edwards and Wesley.

MANAGING MANIFESTATIONS

If you carefully determine something is of God, accept it. If you carefully determine something is of human origin, shepherd people through correction and redirection. This does not mean to attack or shut down anyone. That hurts people. Hurt people sulk, leave, or cause division. Jesus did not authorize us to treat His sheep that way, nor did any other leader of the New Testament. The rebukes in the New Testament are directed at those who willfully disobey and carnally indulge themselves. The response to problem behavior starts with loving correction, redirection, and guidance.

People will ask, "Are these outward manifestations of God?" The answer will always be no. Manifestations are never of God, or of any other spirit for that matter. Manifestations are human responses to the Spirit of God (or on occasion to other spirits), though sometimes they are responses to a strong leader or group psychology. When something good happens, people express happiness. When something bad happens, people express dismay. Some people are demonstrative, while others are reserved or may hide their feelings. Each of these behaviors is a human response to an external situation. We would be unwise to judge people or the spiritual situation based on how they behave.

This is how it is with the Holy Spirit. People respond differently. It depends on personality makeup, what is going on with a person, and what the Lord does to that person. Sometimes a whole crowd of people will respond similarly, whether out of a corporate mentality or out of consistency with what the Holy Spirit is doing. We waste precious opportunities and spiritual blessings if we focus on manifestations. What God is doing inside people is where our focus must be and where lasting fruit will be born.

If a manifestation appears to obstruct the work of the Holy Spirit, call excessive attention to itself, or show signs of being fabricated, calmly and gently move the person involved to another place for private ministry. That person will usually need and respond better to kind clarification and counseling than to confrontation. Until we truly know what is going on in any situation, we would be wise to tread gently. If a person is obstinate and causing problems, then a more confrontational approach is biblical and necessary.

Since outward manifestations are only human responses to the power of the Holy Spirit, they are not worth getting excited or upset about. Unless they are disruptive and hinder what God is doing, we should generally not hinder manifestations. But neither should we encourage or manipulate them. Most people will figure out fake stuff anyway. I have had people swoon as Wesley did (commonly called "slain in the Spirit"), shake, sob, laugh, cry out, flail their bodies about, gently weep, or sit still in prolonged silence. But it doesn't really matter. If anything outward is to happen or not happen, let God be in charge. Always focus attention on what the Holy Spirit is doing in a person's heart.

Some may see manifestations as signs of spirituality, but actually the opposite may be true. They are more likely signs of deep-felt needs, emotional wounds, excitable personalities, and occasionally even demonic reactions to the power of God. I've had excitable people who responded to just about anything. They simply needed to be calmed down. I've had emotionally wounded people who responded more demonstratively than others, because damaged emotions are more sensitive and reactive to the Holy Spirit. I have had people who were unwittingly oppressed or afflicted by demons throw themselves down or utter foul screams or growls, because demons at some point will react to an overpowering presence of God. Demonized people did this before Jesus. I've also had a majority of people who made no outward response to anything. I learned to be careful not to overlook these calm, quiet folks in whom the Spirit was working and who sometimes needed ministry just as much as the others. Don't waste attention on what to do about manifestations. And don't get into fakery by promoting them. Focus on what the Spirit is doing and what ministry each person needs.

You are probably more familiar with the situation where the Holy Spirit does not seem to be working or people do not seem to be responding. But when manifestations do occur, they may scare or put off people unfamiliar with them. In every case a leader must take charge but in a way that expresses love toward the people and sensitivity to the Holy Spirit. The leader or leadership team must

On occasion, revival meetings have extended well into the night and even into the early morning hours! With testimonies, praises, songs sung, altars filling, and lives changed, it is a glorious experience to sense so strongly the presence of God that, at times, I've had to encourage the people to go home to rest.

—E. P.

shepherd people through situations in a way that glorifies Jesus and does not divide His Body.

We may trace the outline for a simple working principle in this 1905 report of the Welsh Revival:

It wisely discerns the Holy Spirit's centrality in the midst of spontaneous exuberance: "One is struck with the simple spontaneity of it all. . . . The meetings, often prolonged through the whole night, seem to conduct themselves. 'Disorder,' one would say. But no: from all accounts it is clear that there is a controlling spiritual power that dominates and directs in all. Everywhere stress is laid upon the personality and operation of the Holy Ghost."[5]

MIND-SETS

Be aware of mind-sets. On one end is the "genteel mind-set"; on the other, the "frontier mind-set." Most of us are somewhere in between. In centuries past the genteel mind-set was often called "Formalist" and the frontier mind-set "Methodist."

The genteel mind-set feels at home in churches where respectability is important. Worship is formal and orderly, with little or no emotion expressed. People of this persuasion have generally been uncomfortable with the more expressive atmosphere of revivalistic meetings.

The frontier mind-set feels at home with worship that is informal. People of this persuasion have generally favored revivals and the emotional demonstrations both of preachers and people who take part in them. Prostrations, rolling, and shaking are accepted and embraced. The uncritical thinking and expressive emotions of people who settled the American frontier were where this mind-set got its name.

When the Holy Spirit operates in your midst, especially if He is being poured out, being aware of these mind-sets, and the spectrum in between, will help you in handling yourself, others, and, if you're the leader, the meeting itself.

JEALOUSY

If the work of the Holy Spirit is great enough to be noticed by other churches, some leaders may oppose the work out of jealousy. The famous pioneer missionary Jonathan Goforth tells of an incident in the 1907 revival in Korea. The story shows how jealousy can cause people to oppose God's work and then come under God's conviction.

Before nine o'clock had struck, that Monday morning, in the Ping Yang high school, the Spirit of the Lord was smiting those boys with conviction. . . . Soon the principal's room was filled with boys agonized over sin. . . . By Friday evening the Presbyterian boys had all come through to victory, but it was clear that something held the Methodist boys back.

It all came out that evening, when about a dozen of the Methodist boys went and pleaded with their native pastor to free them from their promise to him. It seems that this Korean pastor was jealous because the revival had not started in the Methodist church. He got the high school boys to oppose it, and to resist all public confession as from the devil. But by Friday night their agony of mind was unbearable, hence their pleading to be set free from their promise.

With that, the pastor went and flung himself at the missionaries' feet and confessed that the devil had filled him with envy because the revival had commenced among the Presbyterians. . . . By the following Monday the students were right with God, with their teachers and with one another, and the school commenced under the Spirit's control.[6]

You can help prevent jealousy. If you experience a powerful work of the Holy Spirit, it's important to maintain humility before others who have not experienced it. True works of the Spirit are nothing to boast about. Boasting separates. Humility embraces. Humility about what the Spirit has done invites others to receive it as well. Even if you don't boast, some people may still be jealous and reject you. What can overcome that but an embracing humility?

NONISSUES AND THE REAL ISSUE

Remember not to equate external phenomena, especially human reactions to the Holy Spirit's presence, with the genuineness of an outpouring or revival. Human reactions to the Holy Spirit are just that—reactions to the Holy Spirit. They are not the Holy Spirit.

If we equate human manifestations with the Holy Spirit, we inevitably make one of two mistakes: On one side, we might say that if certain manifestations appear, it must be the Holy Spirit, and if those manifestations do not appear, the Holy Spirit must not be active. Manifestations can even be induced, especially when a strong leader has an audience that is hungry for God and susceptible to doing things that help them believe God has come in power.

On the other side, we can reject certain manifestations, thinking they are invalid. Thus we might reject out of hand the Spirit's genuine outpouring or activity. Since manifestations are human reactions to the Holy Spirit, we must be careful not to reject what could be a genuine work of God hidden beneath the exterior hoopla.

The main way to discern what's what is to apply the three universals we discussed in chapter 2. Ask these three questions: (1) Are people burdened to pray? (2) Are people being convicted of sin, and their lives transformed? (3) Is there a powerful sense of God's presence? Applying these three questions to any situation will guide you through most situations. Also remember how Paul, in his letters, discerned the genuine work of the Spirit by associating it with Christlike behavior.

Manifestations of any sort need to be kept in their secondary place. Some people may be still when the Lord does a transforming work in their hearts and minds, while others may get excited. Do not allow anyone to puff up the supposed significance—positively or negatively—of outward manifestations and promote them as meaning anything at all. Of what eternal value are human reactions to the Lord's presence and work? None. If people understand this, they are much more likely to avoid such behaviors unless they truly are of God. With this approach, you have the freedom to keep your focus on what God is doing in your heart and in others' hearts, no matter how they behave.

Remember, "Blossoms are not fruit." Blossoms are nice, but it's the fruit that counts.

> Let us not fear or ignore any of the gifts and manifestations of the Holy Spirit, no matter how extraordinary; but be prepared to expect God to reveal Himself to His people, especially in these last days, in many signal and glorious ways.
>
> At the same time let us not fear to exercise the spirit of discernment and to take ample time and measures to be sure that an alleged work bears the signs of God's approval and control. Let us especially watch lest even good movements become mixed with evil through the lack of discernment or carefulness. Let us not be afraid to exercise proper supervision and control in the Spirit over religious assemblies.
>
> —*A. B. Simpson, "Gifts and Graces,"* The Christian and Missionary Alliance Weekly, *June 29, 1907.*

ABOVE ALL ELSE, WEEP AND PRAISE

If, after asking the three main questions, managing the work of the Holy Spirit still seems complicated, here is a reliable rule of thumb: weep and praise. First, we know from both Scripture and history that repenting and weeping over your own sin or that of others is the most appropriate response to the Holy Spirit's conviction of sin (see for example Acts 2:37-38).

Second, when people repent of sin, exuberant praising and rejoicing naturally follow. The biblical word "hallelujah" literally means "Praise the Lord." Hebrew has seven different words for praise, some of them quiet, most of them exuberant.[7] "Halal" (from which we get "Hallel" and "Hallelujah") literally means "to celebrate in abundant rejoicing." Nowhere does the Bible tell us to worship God solemnly. Everywhere it tells us to "rejoice" and "praise."

These two manifestations of weeping and praising were the primary outward marks of those who were part of the Holiness Revival. They have been central to most revivals, or shall I say, to every genuine revival. Look for weeping and praising in your own life and in your church.

FIRE-KINDLING QUESTION

How do you remember yourself or others reacting to the work of the Holy Spirit? Now look beneath the external manifestations, or lack of them. What did the Holy Spirit actually do in your life or in that of others? Would you commit yourself to seeing things this way?

7

A PROPHETIC CHALLENGE
God's Instrument of Revival— You!

WILL THE SPIRIT OF GOD BREAK INTO OUR MATERIALISTIC, over-scheduled, violent, self-centered, indulgent, unholy world? (Some might add "and churches.") If the God we worship is who He says He is, we can expect His Spirit to break in. Here's the other side— He expects us to be part of it. Throughout history God has chosen to work through normal, unworthy people like you and me. When we consistently say, "Yes, Lord!" I believe God can work through us, no matter what the state of our church or community. And in the process we will be transformed.

SPIRITUAL SLUMPS AND RESURRECTIONS

Timothy Dwight, the grandson of Jonathan Edwards, described the period before and during the American Revolution: "The profanation of the Sabbath . . . profaneness of language, drunkenness, gambling, and lewdness, were exceedingly increased; and, what is less commonly remarked, but is not less mischievous, than any of them, a light, vain method of thinking, concerning sacred things, a cold, contemptuous indifference toward every moral and religious subject."[1] It was just as bad, if not worse, after the war. One preacher described the spiritual state of the Carolinas: "How many thousands . . . never saw, much less read, or ever heard a Chapter of the

Bible! How many Ten thousands who never were baptized or heard a Sermon! And thrice Ten thousand, who never heard of the Name of Christ, save in Curses . . . ! Lamentable! Lamentable is the situation of these people."[2] A French nobleman who made a tour of the States wrote, "Religion is one of the subjects which occupies the least of the attention of the American people."[3] Then in the 1790s the Spirit began pouring out and setting America on fire. Thousands were changed, and the nation responded in what became the Second Great Awakening, which lasted 45 years.

Elmer T. Clark describes the spiritual decline that followed the American Civil War. It infected the churches until some Christians got on their knees enough times to pray down the Spirit.

> At the close of the Civil War . . . there swept over the country a wave of immorality, secularism, and religious indifference. The spirit naturally affected the churches, bringing about what many believed to be a lowered moral tone, compromise with "the world," weakening of the insistence on definite religious experience as a condition of membership, with the consequent influx of unconverted persons into the fold, and a general decline of vital piety and holiness of life. As a result . . . the humbler Christians with emotional temperaments and perfectionist leanings began to feel uneasy, to protest against the abandonment of earlier practices, and to seek wherever it might be found the experience of perfect love.[4]

Not many years later the Holiness Revival surged into full swing. Spiritual conditions today are worse than they were then. How many Christians will go to their knees today? How many feel, as Clark says, "uneasy" enough to persistently besiege the gates of heaven? Will you be one?

Our Worst Enemy

Between the 1920s and 1930s the Holiness Movement's fire gradually subsided in many places. Michael Spence writes, concerning Pasadena First Church of the Nazarene, that while revivalistic meetings went on, the church itself

became quieter and more subdued, apparently becoming increasingly similar to that of many other denominational church services in that era. This was a gradual change and the heightened enthusiasm, emotionalism and freedom of the revival meetings were increasingly seen as strange, odd and even comical by the younger generations of the 40s and on. . . . The emotionalism, sanctification and testimonial claims of the revivals were increasingly being viewed with skepticism. . . . and the younger generation was becoming wary of a holiness blinded to the prejudices being addressed through the civil rights movement.[5]

I think we all agree that the Spirit-filled fervor of the Holiness Movement, as happens with every movement on earth, has subsided. The reasons are multiple and complex, but the remedy is simple. The movement needs reawakening.

Morris Chalfant contends that "we live in a world that is on fire, and there are too few Christians who want to be awakened from their dreams. The lethargy, the sleeping sickness which grips us is far more destructive than any forces which threaten the Church from without."[6] He is talking about the

Although I have been privileged to hold revival services in many good churches, I have yet to find a church that doesn't need revival. Today, some say that the "day of the evangelist" is over. It has been my experience in working altars for nearly two decades, that there are many individuals with serious sin issues in the church. It is alarming to hear that some churches don't see the need for revival services. History reports that most people have been saved and sanctified during a revival or camp meeting. Could it be that just when we think we are doing fine, that in actuality we could never be in greater need of revival in our churches?

—E. P.

church's worst enemy. It's not the devil—we have authority over him and his demons. Other people are not our worst enemy—we are to love them no matter what they do or what spirit influences them. Persecution of the church is not the worst enemy—it normally purifies the church and makes it grow. Financial, relational, and other problems are not the worst enemy. They are symptoms of deeper problems and even serve to bring us closer to God.

Complacency—the calm, secure sense of satisfaction with one's lot in life, the feeling that everything is OK (or at least tolerable) and that there's little need to strive for anything—is perilous to the believer. Anyone who lives a comfortable life or even gets exhausted from a difficult one is subject to complacency. It keeps us content with where we are at in our spiritual walk and hinders us from pressing on in our relationship with the Lord. It prevents us from pursuing or even recognizing God's calling and sidetracks us from getting serious about a lost and dying world. It lulls us into spiritual sleep while the devil may be raging. Complacency is subtle, comfortable, and justifiable. And it is deadly to spiritual life. Complacency is our worst enemy.

I have found only two cures for complacency. One is suffering, and that option usually comes against our will. It's no wonder persecuted Christians are so zealous. The other cure is hunger for God. Call it holy hunger or spiritual thirst; by any name it is the deep desire to know and experience more of God. Remember David's craving for God in Ps. 63. Let it be your craving. Desire God's presence in your life more than anything else, and you'll have no room for complacency.

The Challenge Is Even Greater Today

Literature surrounding revivals of long ago often bemoaned secularism, hardened hearts, pride of sophistication, entertainment interests, and busyness. On the one hand, we must recognize that these problems (and others) have always been part of the human race. On the other hand, the slide toward these psychological and social strongholds against God has only gotten worse. Today we are experiencing a pervasive, societal declaration of independence from God that speaks not only of obvious sin in need of repentance but also of material self-sufficiency, which results in moral apathy and indifference toward God.

We have become little gods. Ps. 82 speaks of God judging "the 'gods'"—people in positions of power. Today people in modern nations commonly do things that once we thought only God could do. Do you feel hot? Turn on the air-conditioning. Do you feel cold? Turn on the heater. Is it dark? Turn on the light. To talk to someone on the other side of the planet, just pick up the phone, even a tiny cell phone, while being propelled down a freeway at once inconceivable speeds. With TV we can watch things unfolding on the other side of the planet. Want to go there? Hop on a plane. Sick? Go see a doctor, or buy medicine to cure your illness. Want to calculate statistics beyond human ability or send instant messages? Turn on the computer, or carry it in the palm of your hand. With molecular-scale technology, the abilities of humankind and our machines will catapult to heights even now inconceivable. Though all these things have their earthly limits, those limits are stretched far enough that most people deceive themselves into thinking they don't need God.

If being like little gods is not enough, we have busyness and distractions. We have the compulsory things of life, but we also make choices of what we see, hear, do, undo, make, break, and play. People fill their lives with every conceivable activity on the assumption that they will somehow feel more fulfilled. They don't want to miss anything. They want to do everything, then wonder why they're tired and stressed. They want to own everything, then groan about their debt. Put all this together and we find ourselves in a world more spiritually challenging than ever before.

When we talk about praying for revival, we can be honest in

saying that the challenge towers higher than ever before. We may have to pray harder and longer, crying out from the deepest depths of our souls. Yet the very problem of contemporary society is also at the heart of why most believers do not pray hard, weep, or cry out. The same godlike self-sufficiency and indifference, even if it's converted and baptized, often infects those who seek the outpouring of the Spirit. Most Christians who pray for the outpouring of the Spirit say their prayer and move on. Casual prayer was never enough before, and it is not enough now.

But that does not have to describe you! You determine what describes you. Whether or not the Spirit pours out on you, you'll still get renewed in the process of seeking Him.

TRANSCENDING THE RAT RACE

If you've read this far, it's a good sign that you really want to see the moving and outpouring of the Holy Spirit. And if you live in the same busy world the rest of us do, you'll often feel torn. Michael Warden says, "We are continually torn between two realities: the reality of the heavenly realm where God's purpose and presence are all that matters and the reality of the physical realm where every little thing seems to matter *right now*."[7] So we ask, what do we do about it? Warden continues, "It's not time management. . . . I needed something more than external discipline; I needed an internal transformation, a new way of looking at things."[8]

"A new way of looking at things" means we must deeply decide what is most important to us. Why are you alive? For what purpose does God have you here? What is earthly life compared with eternal life? You may not be able to escape the rat races of life, but you can transcend them. We start transcending the rat races of life when we firmly establish our top priorities. Transcending becomes a reality when we make choices day in, day out that put God's interests first. These choices must prioritize seeking God before the busy stuff. We inhabit the kingdom of this world, but we live to see the kingdom of God invade this world.

Calling on God

Isaiah 62:6-7 exhorts us: "You who call on the LORD, give yourselves no rest, and give him no rest till he establishes Jerusalem and makes her the praise of the earth." Beyond the actual city, "Jerusalem" also refers to the presence of God among His people. God calls us to call on Him passionately, without ceasing. He knows it's not easy. Second Chron. 16:9 says, "The eyes of the LORD range throughout the earth to strengthen those whose hearts are fully committed to him." Is He strengthening you? He knows you need it to keep going. And He intends to establish His presence among His people.

> Be a warrior not a worrier! To be a person of prayer is a choice, a chosen lifestyle. Becoming a prayer warrior takes discipline. We must train ourselves to be godly. "Train yourself to be godly. For physical training is of some value, but godliness has value for all things, holding promise for both the present life and the life to come" (1 Tim. 4:7-8).
>
> —*E. P.*

Will you be among those who call on the Lord, giving yourself no rest—yet being strengthened by Him? Will you pay the price of making your prayer physical? Will you fast with an Isa. 58 attitude? Will you keep praying until God's presence is powerfully established among His people?

Yes, seeking God will cost you hours of prayer. It will cost you to have a humble, hungry, Christ-focused heart. But this really is not so demanding when your alternative is probably getting caught up in more busywork. When the price of not having more of God is increased anxiety, depression, loss of God's direction, and unanswered prayer, the hours of prayer start looking very good.

Red-Hot "Noiserenes"

Timothy Smith collects the core themes of Phineas Bresee's vision for the Church of the Nazarene as expressed in his sermons and editorials:

> Let the Nazarenes establish "centers of Holy fire" in all the great cities of the nation. Let them actively recruit both ministers and key laymen from those who were losing heart in the crusade to bring back the older churches to the faith of their fathers. Let them extend the largest possible fellowship to every congregation and association of holiness people. Let them stand foursquare against fanaticism, legalism, and sectarianism, even while seeking out and evangelizing the poor. And the glory and glow of their work would attract young men, strong and true, who would help build holiness churches in every corner of the land.[9]

This is not a call to start programs and go through weekly church activities. Bresee was calling for a continuation across the land of the fiery power of holiness that the Holiness Movement lived and breathed and that far too many have lost and substituted with respectability.

In the early half of the 20th century, people used the terms "red hot" and "red-hot religion" to describe early Holiness pastors and evangelists, along with the physical manifestations common in that time.[10] Is the spirituality in your church red hot? How is it that we use the term "traditional" to mean someone who is conservative and restrained? That's not what the early Holiness people were like. Shouldn't a traditional Holiness person be red hot?

How about prayer? When is the last time someone called the police because your prayer meeting was too loud? Student prayers at the altar of Pasadena College (which later became Point Loma Nazarene University) were sometimes "loud and demonstrative with shouting and moaning, many times lasting far into scheduled class periods. During one particularly loud evening prayer service during 1938-39 the neighbors around the college called the police, who came to the campus to demand quiet."[11] I've held plenty of meetings just as loud, and always find them a refreshing encounter with God.

Certainly many people can pray as effectively and with as much fervency and do it with hardly a sound. What's important is their enthusiasm and passion to pour out their hearts to God. That's the tradition we need to recapture from the early Nazarenes —this burning desire to open ourselves up to God. That's what these early Nazarenes were doing; they were just expressing their heartfelt enthusiasm in a very "noisy" way. In fact, people some-times called them—"Noiserenes."[12] Are you ready to be traditional in your enthusiasm? Are you ready to reclaim the red-hot passion of the Noiserenes?

THE WORLD AWAKENS

Think about the results of seeking and embracing the outpour-ing of the Spirit, revival, and awakening from this observation on the First Great Awakening during Edwards's and Wesley's time: "The supporters of the Awakening—Presbyterians, Baptists and Methodists—became the largest American Protestant denomina-tions by the first decades of the nineteenth century. Opponents of the Awakening or those split by it—Anglicans, Quakers, and Con-gregationalists—were left behind."[13] God left them behind. He re-spected their choice and kept moving. They still went to heaven, but they missed heaven when it came to earth. God has been mov-ing across the globe ever since and is still moving today.

China has been undergoing a prolonged awakening. When the Communists took control of the country in 1949, China was home to an estimated 4 million Christians. With almost no missionaries and few trained leaders, China is now approaching 100 million Christians! The church is indigenous and highly charged with zeal for God, miracles, and endless streams of new believers.

Across the Islamic world the Holy Spirit is working in extraor-dinary ways, which we could also call an awakening, never seen before in history. Muslims across North Africa, the Middle East, and South Asia are turning to Jesus in unprecedented numbers. Muslim web sites bemoan the growing numbers of Christians. Many Islamic governments no longer keep statistics on the number of Christians—it's too embarrassing.

South America, once a graveyard for Protestant missionaries and pastors, has been on spiritual fire for years. An awakening has spread across the continent. The church has grown exponentially, and even the Roman Catholic Church has been revitalized.

Generations ago, few would have believed any of these places would experience the power of God this way. Will there be a resurgence of the Holy Spirit across North America? Europe? The world? You are part of that answer.

THE GREATEST REVIVAL CHURCH IN YOUR TOWN

The church sign that stood in front of the Los Angeles First Church of the Nazarene in 1928-34 under H. H. Hooker is still preserved by that church and reads: "The Greatest Revival Church in Los Angeles." Don't you wish you could have been there? Yet what matters now is this: How about your church?

If it's not already, could your church be considered "The Greatest Revival Church" in your town?

What would it take to get there?

Take a serious look and make a merciless inventory of what is stopping you.

No program is worth keeping, no power structure worth preserving, no old tradition or new idea worth propagating if it hinders the outpouring of God's Spirit.

When we have the outpouring, none of those programs, power structures, traditions, or new ideas are as important as they were before. We need more of God! We've had enough of everything else. Haven't *you* had enough?

Think about it. Really think about it. And pray. Whatever it costs, however long it takes, change everything that needs to change. You cannot program, manipulate, fake, or force the Spirit's outpouring. But you *can* offer your own life and inspire others in your church to be an open, ready delivery system. You *can* walk in the footsteps of Josiah, Hezekiah, the psalmists, and believers in the Early Church.

No lip service here. Don't tell yourself or anyone else about how much you want the outpouring of the Holy Spirit if you are not willing to stand in one spot, draw a circle around yourself, and say with all that is within you, "Lord, start a revival inside this circle!" Then humbly and passionately be who it takes to let it spread.

Even if it seems this outpouring might never come, just the process of seeking God will renew you spiritually. That alone is worthwhile. A continual hunger for God is the best thing for anyone's spiritual vitality. Thus, as long as you humbly receive what comes or doesn't come, persistently seeking God is a no-lose proposition. You come out ahead no matter what happens!

You may stumble, have good days and bad days. But remember that God forgives—both you and others. Be persistent! Be stubborn! Otherwise the cold, wet blanket of complacency will douse your passion. Remember that complacency is the worst enemy of the church, and it's everywhere. So find other people with like minds. You will need ongoing encouragement, because churches always have people who say they want the works of God but won't pray or cooperate. Some may fear having their ordered religious worlds shaken up and, without knowing it, can be quite religious in their opposition to God. Comfort zones get shaken up, and organizational power structures get put in the backseat when Jesus moves front and center. This is Jesus' intention for a healthy, Spirit-filled church.

No one and nothing can keep you down when all you want is God! When you die or Jesus returns, only one opinion will be important. It's not your parents', your teacher's, your boss's, or your spouse's, and it's not the church board's. It's God's. If God's opinion is the only one that matters, isn't it obvious that it should be the primary one that matters now? Rather than being concerned about what He thinks of you, simply focus on desiring Him. Desire His will and presence in your life. Do that and His opinion of you will take care of itself. On a large scale, that's called "revival."

Do you believe the Holiness Movement can be renewed? Can you see the Holy Spirit empowering the church? What part is God calling you to play? Will you be faithful and stay hungry for Him? Will you give yourself as His instrument of renewal or revival in your local church?

God can use you. God can work through you. He can work through anybody. Would you say yes to Him? Every day? God will use you, whether in big ways or small. And after He does, and you go to be with Him in heaven, He will invite you into an eternal revival.

FIRE-KINDLING QUESTION

What are you going to do? Will you put the book down and say it was interesting? Or will you go to the next two chapters by Elaine Pettit to get inspired about what God is doing today and then get equipped for doing your part to receive it?

8
LET'S DO IT!
Practical Helps for Prayer

IN 1995, REV. STEPHEN ANTHONY, district superintendent of the Eastern Michigan District, scheduled me to preach their camp meeting the following year. Since this is every evangelist's desire, and since it was my very first camp meeting, I was overjoyed.

My husband, Rick, and I decided to visit the 1995 camp to better prepare for 1996. At that meeting very few responded to the altar call. During our three-hour trip home, my heart was burdened. As we prayed, I asked Jesus, "What are we going to do next year? It will be my very first camp. How will we truly reach the people?"

I sensed the Lord's response. "Prayer strategy" came clearly to mind.

I had my reservations. The prayer strategy is a very involved approach to intercessory prayer. Implementing it in a single church takes work. Applying it to over 80 churches seemed an overwhelming task. Recognizing my desperate predicament, I assured the Lord of my obedience. Then the effort began.

For the next 11½ months, we held cottage prayer meetings, developed fasting teams, trained altar workers, and copied and mailed prayer lists of names to hundreds of nationwide intercessors. The prayer strategy was presented in numerous churches, and the district observed several district-wide fast days.

The opening day for the 1996 camp was only two weeks away,

Pat was one of the thousand seekers at the altar that camp meeting night in Eastern Michigan. She testified to a complete transformation, and her testimony has passed the test of time. Since that camp meeting almost 10 years ago, she has become a faithful church member and prayer warrior. Daily she prays over her home church's directory, revival prayer lists, and over 2,000 other prayer warriors. Only eternity will reveal the lasting fruit and the lives benefited by her effort.

—E. P.

and great anticipation was in the air. In my private prayer time, the Lord moved me to pray fervently for the upcoming meeting and for the people who would be attending—the pastors, board members, delegates, Sunday School superintendents, and church laypeople—those most would consider the "cream of the crop." I knew that if after 11½ months of earnest prayer and fasting, the "cream of the crop" would not listen to the Holy Spirit's pleadings, nor humble themselves with radical obedience, then they might never listen.

I began to cry aloud, praying intensely for the Lord to fulfill His promises in their lives, especially that of 2 Chron. 7:14, "If my people, who are called by my name, will humble themselves and pray and seek my face and turn from their wicked ways, then will I hear from heaven and will forgive their sin and will heal their land." I continued praying till I prayed clear through! I had never held a camp meeting, yet I sensed that God was going to do something amazing.

The people assembled for the evening camp meeting service. I preached, and at the close of the message, Wally and Ginger Laxson began to sing. As the altar was opened, a wall of people came forward from every direction of the auditorium! We began to move back the altars to provide more room for the enormous crowd of seekers. The picture was overwhelming! God had moved among His people in an unforgettable way.

INDIVIDUAL PRAYER COMES FIRST

During one of Jesus' most difficult hours, He turned to those closest to Him and asked them to pray. "'My soul is overwhelmed with sorrow to the point of death,' he said to them. 'Stay here and keep watch.'" Then He walked away, fell to the ground, and prayed. When He returned, He found His disciples sleeping. "'Simon,' he said to Peter, 'are you asleep? Could you not keep watch for one hour? Watch and pray so that you will not fall into temptation.'" Two more times Jesus went and prayed, and two more times He returned to find them asleep. "Returning the third time, he said to them, 'Are you still sleeping and resting? Enough! The hour has come'" (Mark 14:34, 37-38, 41).

Today, we face a most critical hour. Once again, I hear Jesus pleading, "Could you not keep watch for one hour? Watch and pray so that you will not fall into temptation."

Many are unaware of the tragedy taking place before us. Multitudes are slipping into an eternal hell today, almost unnoticed—sadly, even by the church! We face desperate days! And I hear His voice again, "Are you still sleeping and resting? Enough! The hour has come."

The hour for prayer has come! We are engaged in a war (see Eph. 6:10-18), the consequences of which are life and death. Praise God that we are not left helpless or hopeless in this matter. God has provided powerful weapons of warfare (see 2 Cor. 10:4) capable of winning this war, and one of these great weapons is prayer! We need to wake up to not only our *responsibility* of prayer but also our *privilege* of prayer.

Jesus gives us the formula for powerful prayer in Matt. 6:6: "But when you pray, go into your room, close the door and pray to your Father, who is unseen. Then your Father, who sees what is done in secret, will reward you."

Another biblical principle is found in Matt. 6:33: "But seek first his kingdom and his righteousness, and all these things will be given to you as well." It is essential that we give Christ priority status in our busy schedules. When we commit quality time to Him and not "leftovers," we choose to shut out everything lesser to make Him our focus.

We need to realize the significance of serving God in the secret place of prayer. And we need to prepare a strategy for success in this holy endeavor.

First of all, we must set our priorities. Many demands are made on our time. Satan knows that nothing defeats him faster than even the weakest Christian on his or her knees. The enemy will attempt to distract you from your private prayer time. To counteract this, we need to seriously consider what keeps us from prayer. The list may include phone calls, e-mails, family, friends, errands, clients, appointments, exercise, sporting events, television, videos, and so on. Once we recognize Satan's scheme to keep us from this prayer time, we need to make a covenant with Jesus, choosing a specific time in our day for prayer. If an hour a day sounds excessive, imagine putting prayer on the "tithe principle." That would mean that we would be required to pray 2.4 hours in every 24-hour period!

Choosing a daily hour of prayer will help you to leave other things temporarily undone. This is a chosen lifestyle, and it demands discipline. First Tim. 4:7-8 admonishes, "Train yourself to be godly. For physical training is of some value, but godliness has value for all things, holding

> In the busy time that we live, many of us wake up and hit the floor running just to accomplish our daily to-do list. At the end of the day, we often regret our lack of success or fulfillment. If instead we begin our day hitting the floor on our knees, we would far more likely end the day rejoicing over what took place. "He is before all things, and in him all things hold together" (Col. 1:17).
>
> —E. P.

promise for both the present life and the life to come." Paul compares the life of a believer to that of an athlete and states, "Everyone who competes in the games goes into strict training" (1 Cor. 9:25). It takes discipline to keep a covenant prayer time with the Lord, but it brings a great reward!

Once a covenant time of prayer is established, it is important to choose a certain place to pray. This consistent place of prayer will help keep your mind focused. In addition, ask God for "praying grace." This will help you to concentrate and remain focused during prayer. Plead the blood of Jesus over you as you pray, and ask the Holy Spirit to help you know what to pray (Rom. 8:27).

There are certain important things to bring with you to your place of prayer. First, bring your Bible, since prayer is a two-way communication. We should not only give our requests to God but also listen to what He may say to us. I have discovered over the years that His main way of speaking to us is through His Word.

Next, develop a list of names to pray for. These may include family, friends, coworkers, fellow church members and church leaders, city officials, teachers, and coaches, among many others. This is in line with 1 Tim. 2:1-2: "I urge, then, first of all, that requests, prayers, intercession and thanksgiving be made for everyone—for kings and all those in authority, that we may live peaceful and quiet lives in all godliness and holiness."

Create a "picture prayer booklet." Purchase a small photo album, and insert pictures of those for whom you feel led to specifically intercede. My mentor, Gertrude Taylor, regularly prayed using pictures, and I have also found this a powerful tool for prayer.

Bring a prayer journal or notebook to jot down any thoughts the Lord reveals to you. This also is a handy way to record your prayer requests, as well as answers to prayer that you receive. Be careful to always praise Him for such answers!

I cannot overstate the importance of private prayer. Earnest prayer touches the heart of God. Jesus is our Example, and His is (even now!) a life of prayer. Col. 1:17 states that "He is before all things, and in him all things hold together." Like the psalmist, I have found it to be true, "In the morning, O LORD, you hear my voice; in the morning I lay my requests before you and wait in expectation" (Ps. 5:3).

Next we'll move into a plan for taking a church into effective prayer for revival—the prayer strategy.

THE ORIGIN OF THE PRAYER STRATEGY

What is this prayer strategy and why is it so effective? For a greater understanding allow me to reflect back to the beginning.

In the late 1980s my local church, Chapman Memorial Church of the Nazarene in Vicksburg, Michigan, asked me to be their Vacation Bible School director. They explained that if the VBS were to have 100 workers and children combined, it would be deemed a success. This was an overwhelming task, and I had no idea where to begin.

I cried out to the Lord, "What am I going to do, and how will I ever do it?" I felt His clear leading to begin in prayer. Gradually several ideas and insights about prayer came to mind, which I wrote down. With no other plan of action, I implemented these ideas among the Chapman people and they began to pray.

I was warned of the difficulty in recruiting workers. Yet as prayer increased, attitudes changed so significantly that at full throttle we had 150 volunteers in a church of about 300 at the time.

As the VBS planning progressed, we realized the truth expressed in Eph. 6:12: "Our struggle is not against flesh and blood [we are not fighting people!], but against the rulers, against the authorities, against the powers of this dark world and against the spiritual forces of evil in the heavenly realms." It became obvious that victory would come only as the further instruction of the Book of Ephesians was heeded: "Therefore, put on the full armor of God, so that when the day of evil comes, you may be able to stand your ground, and after you have done everything, to stand" (v. 13). Verse 18 finishes by saying, "Pray in the Spirit on all occasions with all kinds of prayers and requests. With this in mind, be alert and always keep on praying for all the saints."

The more the people prayed, the smoother the work went. Soon all workers were assigned an intercessor, or "prayer warrior." We scheduled cottage prayer meetings and organized three divisions of fasting teams. One team committed to fast and pray prior to VBS, one group during VBS, and the third team would fast and pray as a follow-up. We compiled lists of all workers and all VBS children registered. The church people copied, circulated, and prayed over these lists. When specific needs arose, we activated a VBS prayer chain.[1]

As Chapman Memorial's people seriously embraced this prayer strategy, the VBS took on miraculous proportions! As stated before, the church produced 150 workers! During the five days of VBS, 563 children attended and 200 conversions were reported! A 10-week follow-up program was implemented. And on Sunday morning, 798 attended the VBS closing program!

After this God opened the door for me to lead one of the VBS workshops at the 1989 General Convention of the Church of the Nazarene in Indianapolis. As a result, this prayer strategy was introduced to many nations of the world—all because God hears and answers prayer!

The Diversity of the Prayer Strategy

What began with a Vacation Bible School has since grown to encompass district children's camps and crusades, inner-city ministries, revivals, district women's retreats, Holiness crusades, and camp meetings. The prayer strategy's effectiveness has also been proven among various denominations and all sizes and types of churches. It has also stood the test of time, as much of the fruit of the meetings has been fruit that has remained and multiplied.

Why a Prayer Strategy?

I mentioned this earlier regarding individual prayer, but I want to underline it now—we must realize we are involved in a war. In Eph. 6:10-18, Paul draws attention to an unseen world and describes an unseen battle going on in the air: "For our struggle is not against flesh and blood, but against the rulers, against the authorities, against the powers of this dark world and against the spiritual forces of evil in the heavenly realms" (v. 12).

In 2 Cor. 10:3, Paul tells us, "Though we live in the world, we do not wage war as the world does." In verse 4 he refers to "the weapons we fight with." Here Paul is clearly prepared for spiritual warfare when he says they "are not the weapons of the world. On the contrary, they have divine power to demolish strongholds." We are in a war, and the weapons God offers us are potent enough to bring down the enemy.

In 2 Cor. 11:14, the Bible tells us that Satan comes as an angel of light. He doesn't announce his entrance into your life's arena but prefers to enter unannounced. He doesn't want you to be aware that a war is going on right in your midst! He'd rather you be preoccupied with all of the cares of this life so you would miss the whole point! Just as the prophet Joel declared, "Multitudes, multitudes in the valley of decision" (Joel 3:14), souls are hanging in the balance—and they are precious souls! Some are strangers, yet others are your sons, daughters, grandchildren, spouse, and friends—even your very own soul. We must awaken to the reality of our involvement in this war, for the consequences are life and death!

There is no question that God has provided what we need for victory. The question is: "What are we doing with what He has offered us?"

Preparing the Ground for Revival Using the Prayer Strategy

Before revival can take place, the soil needs to be prepared. For this to occur, an earnest prayer effort must be initiated. It is of utmost importance that the twofold goal of all we do remains clear: first, we do it for the glory of God, and, second, for the souls of people.

Prayer Lists

With this in focus, begin by gathering the names of all people associated in any way with your church or organization. Divide this established list into groups of 10 names. Hand these abbreviated lists out to all who will commit themselves to intercede daily for these people.

Some individuals in your church will be willing to pray over your complete list of names. Make sure they are supplied with a list for this purpose.

Prayer lists have often been used by great prayer warriors of the past. Daniel Nash, intercessor for Charles Finney, believed in prayer lists of names in preparation for revival. J. Paul Reno mentions this:

> Nash had remarkable power in prayer and was in the habit of making a "prayer list" of persons for whose conversion he daily prayed in secret. . . . The answers to his prayers sometimes seemed almost miraculous, for he did not confine his "list" to those whom he thought might be reached by the revival, but the most . . . unlikely cases were made the subjects of prayer, with results that were truly astounding.[2]

The Evangelist's Support Network

Before we describe further how the church can join in preparation for revival, it is important to note the benefit of a support network from the evangelist's vantage point. Years ago I realized the need for prayer coverage from both the church's team of volunteers and the evangelist's team. So we began recruiting people to be intercessors for our ministry.

Over the years God has graciously provided us with intercessors, or prayer warriors, throughout the country to pray for our meetings. As of this writing we now have over 2,000. We also have nationwide prayer coordinators willing to teach local churches about the prayer strategy. Some intercessors are also on call for additional prayer through our emergency prayer chain. There are even people willing to pray for the intercessors.

All this support is invaluable to our ministry, and God has done many wonderful things through it.

Additional Prayer Lists

In addition to the names on the established prayer list, have each person, including teens and children of reading age, pray for at least 10 people they know who need revival. If they want, they can write these names on a separate list. There also may be other important meeting-related items to pray for that can also be listed and distributed to the people.

Cottage Prayer Meetings

One month prior to revival, weekly cottage prayer meetings should be held. Rev. Mark Hostetler of Portage Grace Church of the Nazarene in Portage, Indiana, shared that in his 26 years of ministry at Grace, the church had not experienced a genuine revival, although revival services were held faithfully twice a year. This time in preparation, they held 26 cottage prayer meetings, and the church experienced a mighty Holy Ghost revival with full altars every service!

Prerevival Fast

One week before the services, everyone should be challenged to fast and pray one meal daily. One day prior to revival, an all-church fast should be called.

24-Hour Prayer Schedule

Prepare a 24-hour prayer schedule and assign volunteers to pray throughout the day prior to the first revival service. Also at this time put the services on the church's prayer chain.

Special Prayer Room

Every evening, a half an hour before service, a special room needs to be designated for those willing to pray.

6 A.M. Prayer Meetings

One of the most effective tools for a powerful revival is the 6 A.M. prayer meeting in the sanctuary each weekday during the revival. It seems there is a parallel between the people's willingness to move out of their comfort zones and God's willingness to pour out His Spirit.

Healing Service

If there is going to be a healing service during the campaign, call a church-wide fast from midnight the day before until immediately following the actual service.

Prayer Vigil

Sunday afternoons and every night, ask volunteers to spend 30 minutes in special prayer for the next service.

Follow-Up Program

The enemy doesn't take a genuine moving of God's Spirit lying down. Satan will try his best to steal the fruit if given the opportunity. Many times the comment "I wonder how long this revival atmosphere will last" circulates. I believe I have the answer: as long as the church wants it to! At the end of the final service, I share with the people that they need to do their best to commit to doing these things:

- Continuing the early morning prayer times at least twice a week
- Organizing a Saturday evening hour-long prayer time in preparation for the Lord's day
- Transforming the intercessory prayer list of meeting-related items to one listing the needs of their local church

- Enlarging upon the established church prayer list
- Challenging themselves to be faithful in keeping their Matt. 6:6 hour of daily prayer
- Establishing a weekly one-day church-wide fast

Prayer Follow-Up Team

In an effort to preserve the fruit of the revival, have a group of committed volunteers pray through the church list of names. This follow-up intercession is a further protection from the onslaught of the enemy and his scheme to destroy the effects of the revival.

That is the general outline of the prayer strategy. Why not make plans to start using it soon? Who knows what tremendous things might happen if you and others open your hearts to God in this way?

FIRE-KINDLING QUESTION

Which of the individual prayer helps will you apply in your own life? What part will you play in implementing a prayer strategy for revival in your church?

9

REVIVAL EXPERIENCES TODAY
What Is God Doing Now?

FOR YEARS A YOUNG COAL MINER NAMED EVAN ROBERTS yearned to preach the gospel. "One day in 1904 while Roberts was in prayer, God revealed to him that He was going to send a revival to Wales, and that one hundred thousand unbelievers would turn to Christ. . . . Burning with this vision, Roberts sought opportunity to preach, but found none. . . . Finally, after much pleading, the pastor relented.

"'All right, Evan, you can preach following the Wednesday night service,' he said, 'if anyone chooses to stay and listen.'"[1] This 25-year-old coal miner did not appear destined to do great things for God. Yet he had a heart desperate for God. Following the regular service that night, 17 people stayed to hear him.

"The next night more came to hear the young preacher, and the fire quickly spread to other churches. *In the next thirty days, thirty-seven thousand came forward to repent for their sins and receive Jesus. Within five months, one hundred thousand were swept into Christ's kingdom across the country*" (italics mine).[2]

Newspapers began printing names of those being saved. Colleges closed down while students marched to prayer meetings. Men began to form "prayer brigades," in which they would pray, sometimes all night, "for God to rouse other men out of bed, convict them of sin, and save their souls." Other men actually crawled out of bed in the middle of the night to find a meeting where they cried out to Jesus for salvation.[3]

The movement spread to become the Worldwide Revival. Here are a few reports just from America:

In Atlantic City, New Jersey, in a population of sixty thousand, it was said that "not even fifty" refused to come to the Lord Jesus Christ.

In Paducah, Kentucky, the First Baptist Church added one thousand new converts to its roll; the pastor died, reportedly from exhaustion.

In Denver, the mayor declared a day of prayer and by ten in the morning the churches were filled, and another twelve thousand packed downtown theatres and halls.

In Portland, two hundred and forty stores signed an agreement to close from eleven in the morning until two in the afternoon to encourage employees and customers to freely seek God.

In Los Angeles, thousands marched in the street celebrating the coming of the Holy Spirit, and two hundred thousand gathered for a single open-air meeting.

Historians estimate that twenty million people came to Christ while this revival burned in America.[4]

WHY DON'T THESE SAME THINGS HAPPEN TODAY?

I've heard many excuses why such things don't still happen, but the truth of the matter is that we have changed. God has not changed, we have changed! In Heb. 13:8, we are assured that "Jesus Christ is the same yesterday and today and forever." Mal. 3:6 echoes the same thought, "I the LORD do not change." Then what has happened?

In the busyness of the day, there is often pressure to take shortcuts to meet our schedules. In so doing, many have shut out His voice. The enemy will lend any excuse to divert our attention away from prayer. Satan knows that if he can merely keep the people from connecting with God through prayer, eventually he can defeat them. Jesus admonishes us in John 15:5, 7-8 about living in dependence on God: "I am the vine; you are the branches. If a man remains in me and I in him, he will bear much fruit; apart from me you can do nothing. . . . If you remain in me and my words remain in you, ask whatever you wish, and it will be given you. This is to my Father's glory, that you bear much fruit, showing yourselves to be my disciples." For anything spiritual we must depend on the Lord as a branch depends on the vine. J. B. Chapman echoes this, saying, "God always does the best He can for all of us. But His best for us when we do not pray is not the same as His best for us when we do pray."[5] W. J. Harney puts it graphically, "I tell you, we must live upon our faces more and talk less, if the great revivals are to come."[6]

Private Prayer and What God Is Doing Today

Ephesians 3:20 states, "Now to him who is able to do immeasurably more than all we ask or imagine, *according to his power that is at work within us*" (italics mine). We desire to see great and awesome things from God, *but are we willing to stop everything less important in order to plug into Him as our Power Source?*

In Luke 10:38-42, Jesus visits the home of Martha and Mary. Martha is busy with her work, yet Mary has stopped everything to merely sit and listen at the feet of Jesus. Distracted by all the preparations, Martha walks over to Jesus and asks, "Lord, don't you care that my sister has left me to do the work by myself? Tell her to help me!" (v. 40).

Jesus answers Martha by stating that *she* is the problem. "'Martha, Martha,' the Lord answered, 'you are worried and upset about many things, but only one thing is needed. Mary has chosen what is better, and it will not be taken away from her'" (vv. 41-42).

If we were in Jesus' place, wouldn't we have viewed this scenario differently? Wouldn't we have given the distinguished service award to Martha? At least she had something to show for her work! Instead, Jesus honored Mary for what she did in such a way that 2,000 years later we're still talking about it. He said, "Only one thing is needed." What is that one thing? The answer is in Ps. 46:10: "Be still, and know that I am God."

Spending time alone with Jesus was the one thing needed then and the one thing still needed today. It is the central habit of radical dependence on God. Everything else pales in significance to this. If we are to see a significant move of God in our personal lives, families, churches, communities, nation, and world, we must willfully choose to be radically dependent on God.

In our day, many people "pray on the run." Due to the heavy demands on their time, they pray as they go to work, school, church, and so on. It is better than going without any prayer, but it is not "power praying." And our dependence slides from God back to ourselves. From personal experience, I have found a definite difference between this kind of prayer and private "alone with Jesus" prayer. Jesus gives us the formula for power praying in Matt. 6:6: "But when you pray, go into your room, close the door and pray to your Father, who is unseen. Then your Father, who sees what is done in secret, will reward you." E. M. Bounds echoed this: "Much time spent with God is the secret of all successful praying. . . . God does not bestow His gifts on the casual or hasty comers and goers. Much time with God alone is the secret of knowing Him and of influence with Him."[7] All believers should discipline themselves to maintain at least a one-hour daily Matt. 6:6 prayer time.

Great Christian leaders of the past kept this prayer discipline. Many enlarged it. John Wesley spent two hours daily in prayer. Martin Luther said, "If I fail to spend two hours in prayer each morning, the devil gets the victory through the day. I have so much business I cannot get on without spending three hours daily in prayer."[8] Jonathan Edwards was known for praying three hours a day. Charles Finney would advise his preachers that no amount of study would compensate for much time alone with the Lord in prayer. I firmly agree with Bounds, who said, "The preachers who are the mightiest in their closets with God are the mightiest in their pulpits with men,"[9] and also with Daniel Nash: "We refuse to so strive and should not be surprised at the lack of God's mighty stirrings. Is it not amazing that we have no problem with people wearing themselves out in sports for pleasure, work for money, politics for power, and programs for charity, but think it is fanatical to so pray for souls?"[10]

For these reasons, every pastor, evangelist, missionary, and Christian leader should devote themselves to two hours daily of Matt. 6:6 private prayer. May the testimonies of the following pastors encourage you in this endeavor.

"STRUCTURED PRAYER CHANGED MY LIFE, MINISTRY, AND THE CHURCH"

Michael Percell, pastor of Jackson First Church of the Nazarene in Jackson, Ohio, shares this testimony:

> Since [I committed to spend two hours a day] in prayer, I have seen God moving in my life and the life of the Jackson Church. Nine months after the revival . . . we are seeing the attendance on Sunday morning move back over the 300 mark, budgets are being paid, with offerings up at an all time high. We just baptized nine new converts, new ministries are being developed, and I have a peace that I have never enjoyed before in my Christian life. . . .
>
> I challenge every pastor (and layman) to spend at least two hours in prayer. It will change your life and your ministry.[11]

Confessions of a "Prayerless Pastor"

Jim Ballenger, pastor of Harris Chapel Church of the Nazarene in Selma, Indiana, shares his heart:

> My prayer life has always been like a roller coaster. Prayer

has been part of the pastoral ministry, but mostly in a crisis or "professional" mode, i.e., people facing surgery, families facing divorce, etc. Prayer was the invitation to pray at a civic event. It was the pastor prayer time in the worship service. It was visiting another church and being asked to pray over the offering.

I had been so empty for weeks leading up to the [revival] meeting. The problem was I was doing ministry work, but my prayer life was suffering.

On Monday the 14th, God got a hold of my heart and convicted me that I was not a person of prayer. . . . Things changed immediately. I made a covenant with the Lord to pray two hours a day.

Prayer is so powerful and it's saturating my life with God's presence. We have prayer time at the church on Wednesday at 6 A.M. and Saturday at 6 P.M. On Saturdays we walk through every Sunday School room and touch every pew, praying for God to bless and anoint His house and His people. I have recruited a number of prayer partners that hold me up daily. We are fasting a day each week for the needs in our church and the world around us.

I am no longer a "prayerless pastor." There's no turning back, no letting up, and no giving up. . . . Praise His Name.[12]

GREAT THINGS IN OUR DAY

My story is one of God taking "the least of these" and by teaching me to live radically dependent upon Him alone, I have been privileged to see great things *in our day!* But I'm not the only one. Others throughout the world have also witnessed the contemporary work of the Holy Spirit's wonderful outpouring. In the words of others, allow me to share with you some things that happened in recent revivals. Some are from my ministry; some are reports about what God is doing through ministries elsewhere in the world.

A Tremendous Week in Georgia

Here is a report from Curtis Sellers, pastor of Gracepointe Nazarene Church in Loganville, Georgia; this is about a series of meetings of which I was privileged to be a part:

> What a week we had! We started out with packed altars on Sunday morning, Sunday evening, and Monday evening. I thought the response would weaken but it kept going every service. We had two young men that were delivered from pornography addiction. . . . We had a young couple that had only come to our church once for a Christmas production. . . . She came back Monday night and went to the altar and was saved for the first time in her life. . . . We had a gentleman that ran our sound in our children's church that . . . we could never get . . . into a church service. He came to all of the services except Sunday night. He went to the altar on Tuesday night and was gloriously saved. He was weeping and raising his hand in praise to God. . . . He now wants to join our church.
>
> With the fact that most of our people drive one hour to work one way, I thought the 6 A.M. prayer meetings would be very low. We averaged 45 in attendance each morning. . . . The last revival we had we could do no better than an average of 70. . . . We averaged 198 in the evening services of this revival. . . . We had close to 400 in attendance on Sunday morning. I received a phone call . . . our people want to continue the 6 A.M. prayer meetings on Monday mornings, the 24-hour fast each week . . . and a weekly prayer meeting on Saturday from 6 to 7 P.M. Needless to say God did a tremendous work in our church. . . . We give God the glory and praise![13]

A Day of Prayer in South Africa

Here is a snapshot of what God did during a special "Day of Prayer for Africa" in May 2004:

> Reports were received about "weeping men, women being

restored, youth blessing the older generation," and many other wonderful things happening.

This is what happened in Idutywa:

Pastor Peter Barnes spoke on Gen. 1:1-2. Towards the end of his speech three British missionaries walked. They asked to greet the people. They went on their knees and asked forgiveness for what the English did to Africa. "God came down in the house, and people burst [out] weeping before the Lord."[14]

Extended Revivals Today

I am not one to extend a revival lightly, and never without earnest prayer and seeking God's will in His Word. Yet I have had the wonderful privilege of being a part of several outpourings that stretched beyond what was scheduled. Here is one example from July 1994, as reported in the March 1995 issue of the *Herald of Holiness:*

> At one revival a multimillionaire testified that he'd lost everything and now drove a school bus. His first day was so hard, he just wanting to park the bus and cry. But Jesus drew near to him and he was reminded that although Jesus was God, He had taken upon himself the form of a servant and had made himself of no reputation (Phil. 2:5-8). The glory of the Lord filled the room as he spoke!
>
> —E. P.

More than 230 persons testified to significant spiritual victories during a 50-day spontaneous revival in Lexington, Kentucky, last summer. The meetings were sponsored by three Lexington churches: Eastland Park, Gethsemane, and Lafayette.

Evangelist Elaine Pettit was originally scheduled to preach two Sunday services on the July 4 holiday weekend. As the revival developed, the evangelist eventually asked to be relieved of engagements at four churches and two district camps to attend to the spiritual movement.

During the course of the revival, two baptismal services for 36 candidates were held. In addition, testimonies of 15 physical healings were recorded. Visitors came from eight states and various parts of Kentucky to participate in the services.[15]

Paul Whiteford, pastor of Marysville Church of the Nazarene, Marysville, Ohio, testifies of this revival that extended to 16 days:

Our altars were full every service. . . . I have never had the privilege of praying with so many people to be saved and sanctified in such a short time. In fact our altars had seekers at all times of the day and great victories were won!

Revival is still going on. People are making restitution, paying back tithes up-to-date, seeking reconciliation with each other. Our offerings have nearly doubled each week since revival began in March.[16]

What an awesome experience the Marysville revival was! During the revival, a 35-year-old man who had two heart catheterizations within two weeks and needed a heart transplant had his cousin anointed in proxy for him. Soon after, he felt so much better that he decided to return to his doctor. After further testing, he was told that he no longer had a heart problem and would not need a heart transplant! Eight months after the services ended, I spoke with Pastor Whiteford by telephone. The man who had been healed of a diseased heart was well, and more back tithes had come in. Due to the doubling of regular church offerings, they had to have a board meeting to decide what to do with the excess money.

The Spirit of God Poured Out in Saskatoon, Saskatchewan, Canada

God did a tremendous work at a weekend retreat for young people in Saskatoon, Saskatchewan, as this report from March 2003 recounts:

The second night, the service took an unpredictable turn. In fact, before the Spirit of God inhabited the building and us, the only thing that came out of the speaker's mouth was, "First Samuel." In every corner of the room people began experiencing the manifest presence of God. Standing, walking, or even talking became virtually impossible. . . .

. . . We were changed on the inside. We came home with a new perspective on God's love, His presence and His plan. To have an encounter with God and minister to Him with our lives cannot help but bring change to our hungry hearts.[17]

An Outpouring of the Holy Spirit at West Carrollton Church of the Nazarene

Here is a report from Carol Fulkerson of Harrison, Ohio, about a series of meetings I held at West Carrollton. As you will see, just like the outpouring in Saskatoon, sometimes God doesn't need a speaker; He just goes straight to work:

During the revival at West Carrollton, Ohio, God poured himself out mightily upon us. The altars were filled every night and lives were dramatically transformed. . . . Many who were beautifully sanctified early in the week saw six or more others in their own family saved, sanctified, or healed by the end of the revival services. One night after the service, someone told an employee at Waffle House about the great moving of God at the revival. The waitress came in, and without any preaching went up to the altar to be saved. . . .

Sunday, during the second morning service, the Holy Spirit fell powerfully on the first measure of the first praise and worship song! . . . Jeremy sang "Crown Him with Many Crowns" and the altars began to fill again and again. Elaine never got a chance to preach. The service continued for over two more hours with people pouring their hearts out to God at the altar! We estimate over 100 people were sanctified Sunday morning, but there was too much glory to count! Sunday evening again, without Elaine even getting a chance to preach, God began to

move and the service continued for four hours, with testimonies of transformed
lives and the altar filling
again. What a mighty out-
pouring of the Holy Spirit!
Those who were privileged
to be there were over-
whelmed in God's holy
presence! Praise the Lord![18]

> During a revival in Lexington, Kentucky, the children were singing "I Want to Be like Jesus." Then a little girl began to cry. She said, *"I* want to be like Jesus!" When she knelt down to receive Jesus Christ into her heart, nine other children came with her!
>
> —*E. P.*

A Glorious Meeting in New South Wales, Australia

This is what happened on one Sunday in 2002 during a seven-week-long series of meetings at the Narrabri Christian Outreach Centre in New South Wales:

> On Sunday 11th August, God . . . "took over" the meeting. The glory of God swept through. . . . Intercession and travail broke out and repentance flooded peoples' hearts, as the onionskins of denial were peeled away revealing their "real" state of heart before a holy God. The Spirit of the Lord is now moving . . . touching peoples' lives, where there is spontaneity of breaking and weeping as God is revealing, dealing with and healing hearts.[19]

United Methodist Revival

Here is a report from Pastor Michael Wilson, Monroe United Methodist Church, Monroe, Indiana, concerning some meetings I held at his church:

> God has done some mighty works in Monroe, Indiana. A young adult Sunday School class . . . had fallen away from Christ and the Church. Last Sunday, the first since our revival, their classroom was full for the first time in a long time. Practically every member of the class had made a commitment to

Christ during the revival services. . . . a young woman with anorexia was found by Christ and found a reason to live. She had been nearly dead five times. . . . Now she has given her life to Christ. These are just the beginning; many more were led to the Holy One during those services.[20]

Wesleyan Revival

Dean Pierce, pastor of Burt Avenue Wesleyan Church, Coshocton, Ohio, testifies to the results of a revival. God had again graciously allowed me to have a part in this:

> This past Sunday was awesome at church. Revival just continued and nearly 90 percent of our congregation was at the altar. Over ¼th have agreed to fast on Wednesday for our new prayer ministry on Wednesday evenings . . . and have also agreed to pray at least one hour a day, fast every third Sunday, be a part of our warriors in a prayer team, pray for the pastoral staff, and participate in the prayer chain. Our bulletin this Sunday has just as many praises as there are concerns. Amen![21]

REVIVAL IS OURS FOR THE ASKING!

Truly God has done great things, and for these wonderful experiences and for all of the lives radically changed, I shout, "Glory!" And yet, I believe we've only begun to see what God would do if, as Peter Lundell has challenged us, we would be willing to "pay the price in God-hungry prayer for receiving His work."

Although I've shared just a part of God's movings in our midst today, there is still much, much more!

Recently my husband, Rick, and I were visiting Mendell and Gertrude Taylor's graves in Bethany, Oklahoma. The Taylors were two of my mentors to whom I will be eternally indebted. After a time of prayer, Rick and I decided to walk through the cemetery to look at the gravestones. When we came upon C. B. Jernigan's grave, my heart was greatly moved. *Would God "do it again" in our day?*

*Could He use ordinary people—who are radically dependent on Him
—to usher in another awakening?*

I remembered Evan Roberts and what God did. My eyes fill
with tears even now as I envision the possibilities of what God
could do today. Imagine for a moment how it could be:

Once again, joy is in the camp as lives are radically transformed! Our churches are packed to overflowing with people who
have been set free! Marriages are restored. Families are reunited.
Teens are running with the torch. Reconciliation and restitutions
are made. Churches open all night, as people are overwhelmed
with a desire to pray. The lost, unable to sleep, make their way to
the church late at night hoping to find help—and find Jesus!

City newspapers print lists of the newly saved. Colleges close
down. Mayors declare "A Day of Prayer." Businesses close so people
could seek God. Thousands fill theatres and halls to pray because
the churches are full. Two hundred thousand gather for one single
open-air meeting. Imagine 37,000 coming to Jesus in one month's
time and 20 million coming to Christ while revival fires burn once
again!

I asked through my tears, "Would You do it again, Jesus?"
And I heard Him whisper, "Would you?"

NOTES

Introduction

1. Personal interview with Dorothy Davis Cook, Alhambra Church of the Nazarene, September 1988.

2. Bill Bright, *The Coming Revival* (Orlando, Fla.: New Life Publications, 1995), 38.

Chapter 1

1. Lawrence B. Hicks, *This Is That: The Song of the Sanctified* (Kansas City: Beacon Hill Press, 1957), 16-18.

2. John McGuckin, "The Eastern Christian Tradition." In *The Story of Christian Spirituality* (Minneapolis: Fortress Press, 2001), 143.

3. Jeanne Guyon, *Experiencing the Depths of Jesus Christ* (Sargent, Ga.: Seed Sowers, 1975), 128. (Reprint; Original publication, 1685.)

4. Selderhuis, "The Protestant Tradition in Europe." In *The Story of Christian Spirituality*, 185.

5. Richard Riss, *A Survey of 20th-Century Revival Movements in North America* (Peabody, Mass.: Hendrickson Publishers, 1988), 20.

6. William McDonald and John E. Searles, *The Life of Rev. John S. Inskip, President of the National Association for the Promotion of Holiness* (Chicago: Christian Witness Co., 1885), 210-11. Quoted in Melvin Dieter, *The Holiness Revival of the Nineteenth Century* (Metuchen, N.J.: Scarecrow Press, Inc.), 126.

7. *Advocate of Christian Holiness*, III (November 1872), 111. Quoted in ibid.

8. E. A. Girvin, *Phineas F. Bresee: A Prince in Israel* (Kansas City: Pentecostal Nazarene Publishing House, 1916), 138.

9. *The Nazarene* (July 27, 1899), 5.

10. *Nazarene Messenger* (October 31, 1901), 9.

11. Thomas Payne, *Revivals—How Promoted* (London: Morgan and Scott, n.d.), 116.

12. Paul Rees, *Seth Cook Rees, the Warrior Saint* (Indianapolis: Pilgrim Book Room, 1934), 37.

13. *Nazarene Messenger* (March 21, 1912), 7.

14. *Nazarene Messenger* (April 23, 1908), 4.

15. *Nazarene Messenger* (April 12, 1906), 4.

16. *Nazarene Messenger* (September 21, 1905), 4.

17. Ibid.

18. *Nazarene Messenger* (June 21, 1906), 4.

19. Girvin, *Phineas F. Bresee*, 108.

Chapter 2

1. C. L. Thompson, *Times of Refreshing* (Rockford, Ill.: Golden Censer Co., 1880), 17.

2. J. Edwin Orr, "The Outpouring of the Spirit in Revival and Awakening and Its Issue in Church Growth" (self-published, 1984), 4.

3. Ibid.

4. Morris Chalfant, *Trademarks of the Holiness Pioneers* (Kansas City: Beacon Hill Press, 1962), 23.

5. Girvin, *Phineas F. Bresee*, 137.

6. Charles G. Finney, *The Memoirs of Charles G. Finney: The Complete Restored Text*, Garth Rosell and Richard Dupuis, eds. (Grand Rapids: Zondervan, 1989), 34-35.

7. Grace Winona (Kemp) Woods, *The Half Can Never Be Told* (Atlantic City, N.J.: World Wide Prayer Movement, 1927), 21-22.

8. J. Edwin Orr, *Good News in Bad Times: Signs of Revival* (Grand Rapids: Zondervan, 1953), 13.

9. Bernard Bresson, *Studies in Ecstasy* (New York: Vantage Press, 1966). Quoted in John Wimber, *A Brief Sketch of Signs and Wonders Through the Church Age* (Placentia, Calif.: Vineyard Christian Fellowship, n.d.), 40.

10. Quoted in Wimber, *Brief Sketch of Signs and Wonders*, 41.

11. Jonathan Edwards, *A Narrative of the Surprising Work of God* (New York: American Tract Society, 1740), 16.

12. Ibid., 20.

13. Ibid., 28.

14. *John Wesley's Journal* 6:77 (September 3, 1775).

15. *The Nazarene* (July 27, 1899), 4.

16. Chalfant, *Trademarks of the Holiness Pioneers*, 31-32.

17. Jonathan Goforth, *When the Spirit's Fire Swept Korea* (Elkhart, Ind.: Bethel Publishing, n.d.), 8.

18. Ibid., 9.

19. *John Wesley's Journal* 2:203 (May 20, 1739).

20. Jonathan Edwards, *Thoughts on the Revival of Religion in New England*, 1740, 151.

21. Woods, *Half Can Never Be Told*, 23.

22. Quoted in Charles Johnson, *The Frontier Camp Meeting* (Dallas: Southern Methodist University Press, 1955), 135.

23. Dieter, *Holiness Revival of the Nineteenth Century*, 108-9.

24. Chalfant, *Trademarks of the Holiness Pioneers*, 17-18.

Chapter 3

1. Girvin, *Phineas F. Bresee*, 142.

2. Ibid., 136.

3. Riss, *Survey of 20th-Century Revival Movements*, 13.

4. *John Wesley's Journal* 3:23 (June 11, 1742).

5. Ibid.

6. Ibid., 3:153 (April 2, 1786).

7. Quoted in *Christian History* VIII:3 (23): 26.

8. *John Wesley's Journal* 5:305 (December 12, 1742).

9. Ibid., 6:78 (September 10, 1775).

10. Dieter, *Holiness Revival of the Nineteenth Century*, 125.

11. *Christian History* VIII:3 (23): 33.

12. J. Edwin Orr, "The History of Evangelical Awakenings," class lecture, Fuller Theological Seminary, 1986.

13. Finney, *Memoirs*, 239.

14. Chalfant, *Trademarks of the Holiness Pioneers*, 24-25.

15. Charles Ewing Brown, *When the Trumpet Sounded: A History of the Church of God Reformation Movement* (Anderson, Ind.: Warner Press, 1951), 127.

16. The original controversy with Pentecostal churches should be footnoted along with Bresee's position. A story propagated by Stanley Fordham and repropagated by others for years has intensified the Nazarene-Pentecostal split:

> It happened that a sister from Los Angeles, who was associated with a small colored Nazarene church, visited Houston, Texas, and on her return to Los Angeles she talked about a "very godly man" she had met in Houston. These colored saints in Los Angeles were moved to send an invitation to Brother Seymour to hold a meeting in their church. In due time he came to Los Angeles, and he took for his text on the first Sunday morning that he stood in that Nazarene pulpit, Acts 2:4. He said that when any one receives the Baptism in the Spirit according to the original pattern, he will have a similar experience to that which the disciples had on the day of Pentecost, and speak in tongues just as they did on that occasion.
>
> That afternoon, when he returned to this mission, he found the door was locked against him because these colored saints thought he was preaching a false doctrine, and they would not allow him in the mission any longer.
>
> (Stanley Howard Frodsham, *With Signs Following: The Story of the Pentecostal Revival in the Twentieth Century* [Springfield, Mo.: Gospel Publishing House, rev. ed., 1946], 31-32.)

The only problem with this story is that it is not true. The entire thing is made up. Vincent Synan named a Miss Neely Terry as the organizer of that church mission and noted that it was on Santa Fe Street. (Vincent Synan, *The Holiness–Pentecostal Movement in the United States* [Grand Rapids: Eerdmans, 1971], 104, 106.) But Carl Bangs points out that

> the Los Angeles Nazarenes kept meticulous Methodist-like records from the beginning in 1895, and connectional interests were well reported in annual assembly minutes and in the *Nazarene Messenger.* There is simply no record of Neely Terry or any Nazarene church, property, or mission on Santa Fe Street. Synan also wrote that Bresee opposed the Azusa Street meeting because it was "a direct threat to his own congregation." But there is no evidence that Bresee lost members to the Pentecostals or that there was any real contact between his church and their movement (Carl Bangs, *Phineas F. Bresee* [Kansas City: Beacon Hill Press of Kansas City, 1995], 230).

This means that the original rift between Nazarenes and Pentecostals was not as severe as is commonly thought. Bresee was not quick at all to address the happenings at Azusa Street. When he did, he was careful and thoughtful:

> Some months ago, among some of the colored people in this city, re-inforced with some whites, there began something which was called the "gift of tongues." . . . The professed gift of tongues was not the only peculiarity of the meetings, but much physical exercise of various kinds, with laying on of hands. The meetings attracted some attention, especially among that class of people who are always seeking some new thing. . . .
>
> The speaking in tongues has been a no-thing—a jargon, a senseless jumble, without meaning to those who do the mumbling, or to those who hear. Where in a few instances the speaker or some other one has attempted to interpret, it has usually been a poor mess. . . .
>
> People who have the precious, satisfactory experience of Christ revealed in the heart by the Holy Spirit, do not hanker after strange fire, nor run after every suppositional gift, nor are they blown about by every wind of doctrine (*Nazarene Messenger* [December 13, 1906], 6).

To the early Nazarenes, then, the supposed gift of tongues was a nonissue, and rightly so. For that is how Paul treats it in 1 Cor. 14. But what was a nonissue to the Church of the Nazarene and other Holiness churches, the early Pentecostals made into a big issue, who it seems looked at outward manifestations more than what God was doing in people's hearts. By 1912 Holiness churches felt forced to take a position.

17. Orr, "History of Evangelical Awakenings."

18. Riss, *Survey of 20th-Century Revival Movements*, 24.

19. Chalfant, *Trademarks of the Holiness Pioneers*, 30-31.

20. *Transformations II* [video]. The Sentinel Group, 2001. Duncan Campbell corroborates part of this testimony:

> God was beginning to move, the heavens were opening, we were there on our faces before God. Three o'clock in the morning came, and GOD SWEPT IN. About a dozen men and women lay prostrate on the floor, speechless. Something had happened; we knew that the forces of darkness were going to be driven back, and men were going to be delivered. We left the cottage at 3 a.m. to discover men and women seeking God. I walked along a country road, and found three men on their faces, crying to God for mercy. There was a light in every home, no one seemed to think of sleep. (Quoted in Colin C. Whittaker, *Great Revivals* [Springfield, Mo.: Gospel Publishing House, 1984], 183.)

21. *John Wesley's Journal* 2:202 (May 20, 1739).

22. Edwards, *Thoughts on the Revival of Religion*, 152.

23. Quoted in Keith Hardman, "The Return of the Spirit: The Second Great Awakening." In *Christian History* VIII, No. 3 (23): 25.

24. Finney, *Memoirs*, 318.

25. George Davis, "Thirty-Four Thousand Conversions in Wales." In *The Great Revival in Wales.* S. B. Shaw, ed. (Chicago: S. B. Shaw, 1905), 37.

26. G. Campbell Morgan, "Lessons of the Welsh Revival." In *The Great Revival in Wales.* S. B. Shaw, ed. (Chicago: S. B. Shaw, 1905), 98.

27. Ruth Tucker, *From Jerusalem to Irian Jaya: A Biographical History of Christian Missions* (Grand Rapids: Zondervan, 1983), 269-73.

28. Riss, *Survey of 20th-Century Revival Movements,* 14.

29. Orr, *Good News in Bad Times,* 29.

30. Riss, *Survey of 20th-Century Revival Movements,* 25.

31. Timothy Smith, *Called unto Holiness* (Kansas City: Nazarene Publishing House, 1962), 122.

32. J. Edwin Orr, *The Restudy of Revival and Revivalism* (Pasadena, Calif.: Fuller School of World Mission, 1981), 7.

Chapter 4

1. For a concise, biblical explanation of this, see George Eldon Ladd, *A Theology of the New Testament* (Grand Rapids: Eerdmans, 1974), 68-69.

2. See, for example, Exod. 31:1-3 and 35:31 with Bezalel and Oholiab. The Spirit also "came upon" people; for example, Num. 11:17-25; Judg. 3:10; 6:34; 11:29; 14:6, et al.; 1 Sam. 10:10; 16:13; 19:20; 1 Chron. 12:18; 2 Chron. 15:1; 20:14; 24:20. One could convincingly argue theologically that Moses and the prophets were filled with the Spirit or at least had the Spirit come upon them in this way.

3. When the Tabernacle was built, it then became the tent of meeting in Exod. 40:1.

Chapter 5

1. Charles G. Finney, *Lectures on Revivals of Religion* (New York: Fleming H. Revell Co., 1868), 13.

2. C. E. Matthews, *A Church Revival* (Nashville: Broadman Press, 1955), 55.

3. Chuck Millhuff, *The Revival Meeting in the Twentieth Century* (Kansas City: Beacon Hill Press of Kansas City, 1976), 65-90.

4. Stephen Manley and Michael Ross, *Revival Preparation Guidebook: Pastor and General Chairman* (Kansas City: Beacon Hill Press of Kansas City, 1982), 13.

5. Hicks, *This Is That,* 12-13.

6. Ibid., 13.

7. Ibid., 13-14.

8. Quoted in Chalfant, *Trademarks of the Holiness Pioneers,* 25.

9. J. Paul Reno, *Daniel Nash: Prevailing Prince of Prayer* (Asheville, N.C.: Revival Literature, 1989).

10. Charles G. Finney, *Reflections on Revival* (Minneapolis: Bethany Fellowship, 1979), 14.

11. William McLoughlin, *Revivals, Awakenings, and Reform* (Chicago: University of Chicago Press, 1978), 151.

12. Timothy Smith, *Called unto Holiness* (Kansas City: Beacon Hill Press, 1962), 235.

13. *The Nazarene* (July 27, 1899), 4.

14. For more information on fasting, see Bill Bright, *The Coming Revival: America's Call to Fast, Pray, and "Seek God's Face"* (Orlando, Fla.: New Life Publications, 1995).

Chapter 6

1. Edwards, *Thoughts on the Revival of Religion*, 150-51.
2. *John Wesley's Journal* 2:221-22 (June 15, 1739).
3. *John Wesley's Journal* 2:202 (May 20, 1739).
4. *John Wesley's Journal* 4:394 (June 24, 1760).
5. A report in "Bright Words." In *The Great Revival in Wales*, ed. S. B. Shaw (Chicago: S. B. Shaw, 1905), 65-66.
6. Jonathan Goforth, "When the Spirit's Fire Swept Korea" (Elkhart, Ind.: Bethel Publishing, n.d.), 18.
7. Hebrew words for "praise" used in the Old Testament:
Towdah: "the lifting of hands," "to bow, prostrate" (Ps. 100:4)
Yadah: "to extend the hand," "to serve" (Ps. 138:1)
Barak: "to bless" (Ps. 103:1-2)
Halal: "to celebrate," "Hallelujah" (Ps. 150)
Zamar: "to touch the strings" (Ps. 92:1)
Tehillah: "the spontaneous song of one's spirit" (Ps. 22:3)
Shabach: "to shout over the presence of God" (Ps. 117:1)

Chapter 7

1. Quoted in *Christian History* VIII:3 (23), 27.
2. Ibid., 24.
3. Ibid.
4. Elmer T. Clark, *The Small Sects in America* (New York: Abingdon Cokesbury, 1950), 71.
5. Michael Spence, "The First Nazarene Church of Pasadena: A Heritage of Prayer and Revival" (Unpublished paper, Fuller Theological Seminary, April 12, 2002), 12-13. Information is based on multiple personal interviews at Pasadena First Church of the Nazarene and with Nazarene Headquarters archives, January through February 2002.
6. Chalfant, *Trademarks of the Holiness Pioneers*, 38.
7. Michael Warden, "A Non-Monk's Guide to Practicing the Presence of God." In *Discipleship Journal*, No. 135 (May/June 2003), 56.
8. Ibid.
9. Smith, *Called unto Holiness*, 130-31.
10. Spence, "First Nazarene Church of Pasadena," 11.
11. Ronald B. Kirkemo, *For Zion's Sake: A History of Pasadena/Point Loma College* (San Diego: Point Loma Press, 1992), 150.
12. Spence, "First Nazarene Church of Pasadena," 9.
13. "Religion and the Founding of the American Republic," A Library of Congress Exhibition, 1998, 6-7.

Chapter 8

1. For further study order *Ideas for a Successful Vacation Bible School*, Elaine Pettit, www.elainepettitministries.org.

2. Reno, *Daniel Nash*, 19.

Chapter 9

1. Bright, *Coming Revival*, 79. Used by permission.

2. Ibid., 80.

3. Ibid., 80-81.

4. Ibid., 82.

5. D. Shelby Corlett, *Spirit-Filled: The Life of the Rev. James Blaine Chapman, D.D.* (Kansas City: Beacon Hill Press, 1945), 189.

6. W. J. Harney, *Praying Clear Through* (Salem, Ohio: Allegheny Publications, 1988), 32.

7. E. M. Bounds, *E. M. Bounds on Prayer* (New Kensington, Pa.: Whitaker House, 1997), 485.

8. Ibid., 486.

9. Ibid., 481.

10. Reno, *Daniel Nash*, 15.

11. Mike Percell, Letter to the author (October 30, 2002).

12. Jim Ballenger, Letter to the author (October 19, 2002).

13. Curtis Sellers, Letter to the author (February 2004).

14. Quoted from Transformation Africa, "Day of Prayer 2004," http://www.transformationafrica.com (accessed November 30, 2004).

15. "Special Outpouring in Kentucky." In *Herald of Holiness* (March 1995), 40.

16. Paul Whiteford, Letter to the author (May 2, 1997).

17. Quoted from Jenna Baird, "Outpouring in Saskatoon, Canada," Open Heaven, http://www.baspub.com/connected/report.asp?id=162 (accessed November 30, 2004).

18. Carol Fulkerson, Letter to the author (February 23, 1998).

19. Quoted from Margaret O'Connor, "Narrabri Nsw—Seven Weeks of God's Presence," Open Heaven, http://www.baspub.com/connected/report.asp?id=124 (accessed November 30, 2004).

20. Michael Wilson, Letter to the author (August 13, 1998).

21. Dean Pierce, Letter to the author (May 4, 2003).

If you would like to contact either Peter Lundell
or Elaine Pettit, please log on to
Lundell.ws for Peter Lundell
ElainePettitMinistries.org for Elaine Pettit